Excel 2019 Macros and VBA

An Introduction to Excel Programming

NATHAN GEORGE

Copyright © 2019 Nathan George

ISBN: 978-1-9162113-4-6

CONTENTS

INTRODUCTION

Welcome to *Excel 2019 Macros and VBA*. As you probably already know, you can use a macro to automate any task that you can perform manually in Excel. Maybe you regularly format a set of data for presentation purposes, or you want to automate some of the repetitive data-crunching tasks you carry out. You can create a macro that does this automatically so that you don't have to go through the repetitive and time-consuming process each time. Macros enable you to work more efficiently and with fewer errors.

After reading this book, you will have all the tools to create your own macros to automate any task that you can manually perform in Excel. You will be able to open your macros in the Visual Basic Editor to make enhancements or fix errors. You'll understand the Excel object model and how to take advantage of it in creating custom solutions for your data. You will be able to write your own user-defined functions using Visual Basic for Applications (VBA) and save them as Excel Add-ins.

Also included in the book, are several readymade macros which you can use directly in your own workbooks or use as a base from which to create your own macros to perform various tasks.

Who Is This Book For?

This book is for you if you're an intermediate to advanced Excel user and you want to learn how to create VBA procedures to automate tasks in Excel. Maybe, you also want to be able to create your own user-defined functions to perform certain calculations for which there are no dedicated built-in Excel functions.

Unlike other programming books that you might have seen, this book doesn't assume you have any programming experience. You don't need to have even written any programming code in your life because we'll start from the basics.

As the title implies, this is a book about using macros and VBA to extend the power of Excel. It's not a general-purpose Excel book. To stay focused on macros and VBA, I'm assuming you're already competent with Excel. If you need a general-purpose Excel book, you can check out my Excel 2019 Basics or Excel 2019 Advanced Topics books.

Excel 2019 Macros and VBA is not an in-depth book on the VBA programming language. It's a vast language and there is only so much a modest-sized book can cover. So, the focus is on the essentials you need to get you started in creating VBA solutions, and to provide solid foundations on which you can build your experience through use. If you're already experienced in VBA, then this book is not for you.

How to Use This Book

Excel 2019 Macros and VBA can be used as a step-by-step training guide as well as a reference manual that you come back to from time to time. If you're completely new to Excel programming, then it is recommended that you read the chapters in sequential order. This is because some topics you'll encounter in later chapters would be based on topics covered in earlier chapters.

If you're already experienced in recording Excel macros, then you can skip to the chapters that cover VBA programming.

Assumptions

The software and hardware assumptions made when writing this book is that you already have Excel installed on your computer (Excel 2013, Excel 2016, or Excel 2019) and that you're working on a Windows 10 computer.

If you're running Excel on a Mac, then simply substitute any Windows keyboard commands mentioned in the book for the Mac equivalent.

Source Code

All code examples in the book are available as downloadable text files. To run a piece of code, you'll need to copy and paste the code in your project in the Visual Basic Editor. You can download the files from the following location:

https://www.excelbytes.com/excel-vba-download

Note:

- Type the URL in your Internet browser's address bar and press Enter to navigate to the download page. If you encounter an error, double-check that you have entered all characters in the URL correctly.

- The files have been zipped into one download. Windows 10 comes with the functionality to unzip files. If your OS does not have this functionality, you'll need to get a piece of software like WinZip or WinRAR to unzip the file.

- If you are having any problems downloading these files, please contact me at **support@excelbytes.com**. Include the title of this book in your email, and the practice files will be emailed directly to you.

What is the Difference Between Macros and VBA?

An Excel macro is a recorded set of instructions stored in Visual Basic for Applications (VBA) code. The VBA programming language was developed by Microsoft as a tool to control and automate Microsoft Office applications.

The difference between Excel macros and VBA programming can be fuzzy because macros are stored as VBA procedures, but not all VBA procedures are macros. For example, you can create Function procedures in VBA that are not used like macros.

You don't necessarily need to have VBA programming experience to record and run simple Excel macros. But to write the macros directly in VBA, or to edit a recorded macro, you need to be familiar with the VBA programming language. On some occasions, the process of creating macros will involve editing the generated code to change how the macro behaves or to fix errors. VBA gives you more flexibility and power to control Excel than the macro recorder affords.

Another benefit of VBA is the ability to create your own custom functions (also known as user-defined functions). This book covers how to create your own user-defined functions as well as how to save a function as an Excel add-in.

1. RECORD AND RUN MACROS

There are multiple ways you can create macros in Excel 2019. The most accessible method is to use Excel's macro recorder to record your actions as you perform various tasks in the worksheet. With this method, you don't need any programming skills.

In this chapter, we will cover:

- The different locations where you can store your macro.
- The three ways you can start the macro recorder in Excel.
- A walkthrough of recording your first macro with an example.
- How to playback your recorded macro.
- Saving your worksheets properly so that your changes are not lost.

Displaying the Developer Tab

Before we start, you need to add the **Developer** tab to your Excel Ribbon (if you don't have it). A default installation of Excel does not add the Developer tab. To work with macros and the Visual Basic Editor, it is much easier to access the command buttons from the Developer tab.

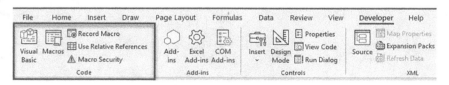

If you don't have the **Developer tab** on your Ribbon, follow the steps below to add it to the Ribbon:

1. Right-click anywhere on the Ribbon (below the buttons) and select **Customize the Ribbon**. Excel opens the **Customize the Ribbon** pane in the Excel Options dialog box.

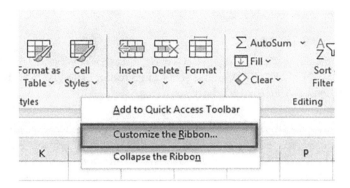

Note: You can also open the Excel Options dialog box by navigating to **File > Options > Customize Ribbon**.

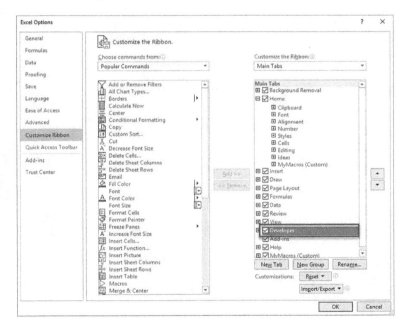

2. On the right side of the Customize the Ribbon pane, ensure **Main Tabs** is selected in the drop-down list. Check the **Developer** check box and then click **OK**.

Where to Store Your Macro

The macro that you create can be stored in the following locations:

- The current workbook.

- A new workbook.

- A globally available Personal Macro Workbook named PERSONAL.XLSB (which is stored in a folder called XLSTART in the AppData folder for Excel on your PC).

When you store your macros in the Personal Macro Workbook, it gives you a central repository for all your macros, which makes it easier to manage. Whenever you open an Excel workbook, Excel also opens the Personal Macro Workbook in hidden mode. This makes the macros stored in it ready and available to be run from other workbooks.

When recording a macro, you get to choose where you want to save the macro, what to name the macro, and what shortcut keys to assign to the macro. When assigning shortcut keys to run the macro, you can assign the **Ctrl** key plus a letter from A to Z, or the Ctrl+Shift keys plus a letter from A to Z. For example, Ctrl+M or Ctrl+Shift+M.

There are some shortcut keystrokes you can't assign, for example, Ctrl+ (any number) or Ctrl+ (a punctuation mark). Also, you should avoid using known Windows shortcut keys like Ctrl+C or Ctrl+V (that is the shortcut keys for copy and paste).

How to Start the Macro Recorder

There are three ways you can start the macro recorder in Excel 2019:

- **From the Status bar**

  On the Excel Status bar, click the **Record Macro** button (bottom left of the screen, next to the Ready indicator). Having the Record Macro button on the status bar is convenient because it means you don't have to switch from your current tab on the Ribbon to start and stop the recording.

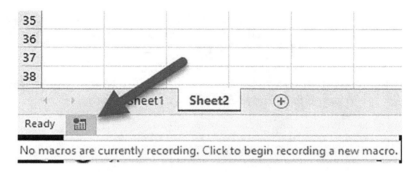

- **From the View tab**

  On the **View** tab, click **Macros** and select **Record Macro** from the drop-down menu.

- **From the Developer tab**

  On the **Developer** tab, click the **Record Macro** command button.

View tab macro options

On the **View** tab of the Ribbon, the **Macros** button has three options on its drop-down list (you can also find these options as command buttons in the Code group in the Developer tab):

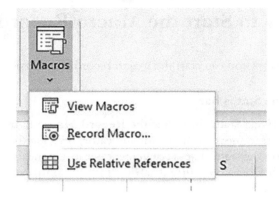

- **View Macros**: This opens the **Macro** dialog box which enables you to select and run a macro that has already been recorded. You can also choose to edit macros from here.

- **Record Macro**: This opens the **Record Macro** dialog box which allows you to define settings for the macro you want to record and then start the macro recorder.

- **Use Relative References**: This setting, which you can turn on before recording a macro, uses relative cell references when recording macros. Using relative cell references makes the macro more versatile because it enables you to run it anywhere on the worksheet rather than where it was originally recorded.

Recording a Macro

In the following example, we'll walk through recording a macro that carries out the following tasks:

- Enters the text "Microsoft Excel Macros".
- Increases the font to 14 points.
- Bolds the text.
- Autofits the column width so that the text does not flow into other columns.

To start recording the macro, do the following:

1. Open an Excel workbook and a blank worksheet. On the **View** tab, click the drop-down button of the **Macros** button (not the command button itself), then select **Use Relative References** from the menu.

2. On the **View** tab, click the drop-down button of the **Macros** button and click **Record Macro**. This will open the **Records Macro** dialog box.

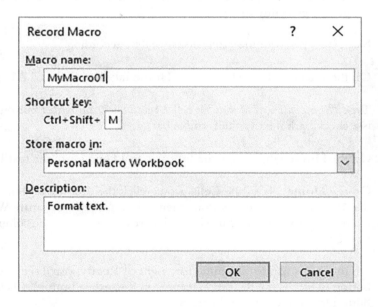

3. In the **Macro Name** field, enter the name of the macro, for example, MyMacro01.

4. For the **Shortcut key**, hold down the Shift key and press M. This will enter Ctrl+Shift+M for the shortcut key. This is the keystroke that you can use to run the macro. You can use other key combinations but avoid using popular Windows shortcut keys.

   Note: The shortcut key is optional, and you don't necessarily need to assign one to every macro you create.

5. In the **Store macro in** drop-down list, select **Personal Macro Workbook**. This ensures that the macro is saved in the global PERSONAL.XLSB workbook and not the current workbook.

6. In the **Description** box, you can enter a brief description of the macro. This is optional, but if you're creating a lot of macros it would be a good idea to enter a description for each macro to make maintaining the macros easier.

7. When you're done, click **OK** to start recording.

   The Record Macro box is closed. On the status bar, next to Ready, you'll see a small square button which is the indicator that the macro recorder is currently running.

   Next, we'll perform the Excel tasks we'll be recording.

8. On the Excel Ribbon, click on the **Home** tab then click cell **A1**.

9. Type *"Microsoft Excel Macros"* in cell A1 and click the **Enter** button (this is a checkmark next to the formula bar).

10. On the **Home** tab, change the font size to 14 and make the text bold.

11. On the **Home** tab, in the **Cells** group, click the drop-down button of the **Format** command button, then select **Autofit Column Width** from the drop-down menu. This will increase the size of the column to fit the text.

12. On the status bar, to the immediate right of **Ready**, you'll see a square button (which is the Record Macro/Stop Recording button). Click that button to stop recording the macro.

With that, your macro recording has been completed. Next, we'll run the macro.

Running a Macro

After recording a macro, you need to test it by running it from the Macro dialog box.

1. Click on any cell in the worksheet area or where you want to insert the text.

2. On the **View** tab of the Ribbon, click the **Macros** command button. Alternatively, on the **Developer** tab, in the **Code** group, click the **Macros** button.

   Excel opens the **Macro** dialog box which has a list of all the macros you have created in the macro name list box.

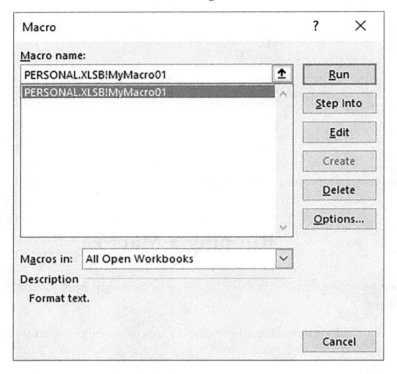

3. Ensure **All Open Workbooks** is selected in the **Macro in** dropdown list.

4. Select the macro in the list box and click the **Run** button. For the macro we created in this example, the name is *PERSONAL.XLSB!MyMacro01*.

   The macro will reproduce the text *"Microsoft Excel Macros"* in the active cell with the text size set to 14, bolded, and the column widened to fit the text.

   Note that the *PERSONAL.XLSB* prefix indicates that the macro was saved in the Personal Macro Workbook.

Tip: If you assigned a shortcut keystroke to the macro, for example, Ctrl+Shift+M, you can just press those keys to automatically run the macro without needing to open the Macro dialog box.

It is best to test a macro in a new worksheet (or a different range in the current worksheet) as you want to see if the macro replicates the actions you performed when recording it.

If you run the macro in a worksheet with existing data, there is a risk that the macro will overwrite your existing data or formatting. To ensure that you don't mistakenly overwrite data, always test the macro in a new worksheet. Only run the macro against actual data when you're satisfied that the macro is working as it should. For example, you may create a macro that adds formatting to existing data. In such cases, ensure you test the macro first against test copies of the data before running it against your live data.

Saving Your Macro

If you stored the macro as part of the current workbook, click the **Save** button on the Quick Access Toolbar to ensure the macro is saved and available the next time the workbook is opened. Even if you have AutoSave set to On, you have to explicitly save your worksheet to ensure your macros are saved.

If you stored your macro globally in the Personal Macro Workbook, you have to save it when you exit Excel. When you try to exit Excel, a dialog box will appear asking you if you want to save the changes you made to the Personal Macro Workbook. Click the **Save** button to save your macro as you close down Excel. This is a very important step because if you close Excel without saving it here, the macro will be discarded.

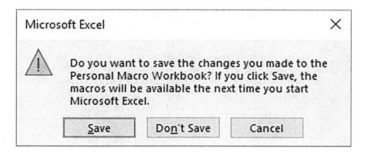

2. ABSOLUTE REFERENCE VS RELATIVE REFERENCE MACROS

Excel cell references are relative references by default, but for recording macros, absolute references are used by default. Relative reference means, when the cell reference is copied across multiple cells, they change based on the relative position of columns and rows. Absolute cell referencing, on the other hand, doesn't change when you copy a formula containing the reference to another cell. For example, the cell reference A3 means the row and column have been set to absolute.

Note: The difference between absolute reference and relative reference in relation to Excel formulas is covered in detail in my *Excel 2019 Basics* book. In this chapter, the focus will be on how using absolute and relative references will affect the behaviour of your macros.

In this chapter, we will:
- Create and run a macro using the absolute reference setting.
- Create and run a macro using the relative reference setting.
- Examine the differences between both types of macros.

With absolute cell referencing, the macro recorder will store specific cell references as part of the code instructions. For example, if the macro was recorded in range A2:A5 in one worksheet, when you run it in any worksheet, it will only perform the tasks in that range.

If you want the macro to perform the tasks in any range in a worksheet, you need to enable the **Use Relative Reference** setting on the **View** or **Developer** tabs of the Ribbon before you start recording the macro. With the reference type set to Relative, the macro will perform the actions relative to the active cell when the macro was started.

To demonstrate this, we will record two macros, one using absolute referencing and the other using relative referencing.

Absolute Reference Macro

In this example, we will create a Macro to calculate a simple total of some figures.

▲	A	B	C	D	E	F
1	**Branch 1**				**Branch 2**	
2	Sales Person	Sales			Sales Person	Sales
3	Carol Rhodes	$4,661.00			Roosevelt Carlson	$4,465.00
4	Silvia Gutierrez	$1,993.00			Wilbert Hudson	$4,561.00
5	Eileen Tucker	$1,860.00			Kathy Steele	$1,272.00
6	Nora Rogers	$1,497.00			Elsie Valdez	$4,794.00
7	Doug Simpson	$1,505.00			Ricardo Barnes	$2,304.00
8	Ashley Hernandez	$1,613.00			Jessie Mcdaniel	$1,251.00
9	Orlando Foster	$4,305.00			Gertrude Houston	$2,595.00
10	Bernice Soto	$3,227.00			Alberta Estrada	$4,071.00
11	Holly Burton	$4,473.00			Darin Coleman	$4,680.00
12	Heather Blair	$2,632.00			Antonia Crawford	$1,590.00
13						
14						
15						

We will record a macro that sums up cells B3:B12 in the data above.

1. On the **Developer** tab, in the **Code** group, click the **Record Macro** button.

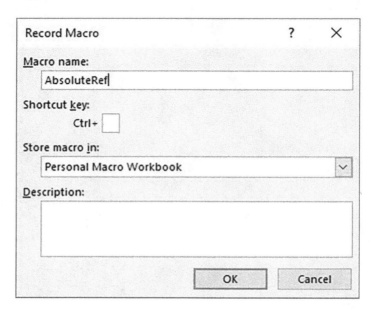

2. In the **Macro Name** field, enter the name of the macro, for example, *AbsoluteRef*.

3. In the **Store macro in** drop-down list, select **Personal Macro Workbook** (if it's not already selected).

4. Click **OK** to start recording.

   At this point, Excel is recording your actions. Carry out the following steps:

5. Select cell A14 and type **Total** in the cell.

6. Select cell B14 and type **=SUM(B3:B12)**.

7. On the **Developer** tab, click **Stop Recording** to stop recording the macro.

The formatted worksheet should now look like the figure below.

	A	B	C	D	E	F
B14			f_x		=SUM(B3:B12)	
1	Branch 1				Branch 2	
2	Sales Person	Sales			Sales Person	Sales
3	Carol Rhodes	$4,661.00			Roosevelt Carlson	$4,465.00
4	Silvia Gutierrez	$1,993.00			Wilbert Hudson	$4,561.00
5	Eileen Tucker	$1,860.00			Kathy Steele	$1,272.00
6	Nora Rogers	$1,497.00			Elsie Valdez	$4,794.00
7	Doug Simpson	$1,505.00			Ricardo Barnes	$2,304.00
8	Ashley Hernandez	$1,613.00			Jessie Mcdaniel	$1,251.00
9	Orlando Foster	$4,305.00			Gertrude Houston	$2,595.00
10	Bernice Soto	$3,227.00			Alberta Estrada	$4,071.00
11	Holly Burton	$4,473.00			Darin Coleman	$4,680.00
12	Heather Blair	$2,632.00			Antonia Crawford	$1,590.00
13						
14	Total	$27,766.00				
15						

Testing the Macro

To test the macro, delete the Total row and carry out the following steps to run the macro:

1. On the **Developer** tab, in the **Code** group, click the **Macro** command button to open the Macro dialog box.

2. Select and run the macro you've just created. For this example, the macro name would be PERSONAL.XLSB!AbsoluteRef.

If all goes well, the macro plays back your actions by entering the total. The issue with this macro is that we can't make the macro work on our second table, **Branch 2**, no matter how hard we try. This is because we recorded it as an absolute reference macro.

To find out what's going on here, we need to examine the source code of the macro.

1. On the **View** tab, click the **Unhide** command button.

2. Select PERSONAL.XLSB in the list box and click on OK to unhide the workbook.

3. Minimise the PERSONAL.XLSB file and go back to the workbook with your data table.

4. On the **Developer** tab, click the **Macro** command button to open the Macro dialog box.

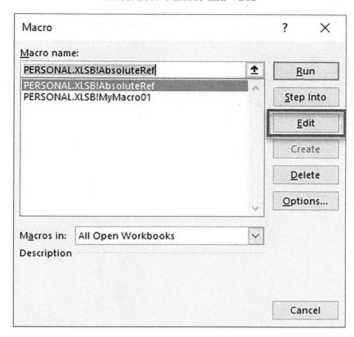

5. Select the PERSONAL.XLSB!AbsoluteRef macro and click the **Edit** button.

    This will open the **Visual Basic Editor** and display the code that was generated when you recorded your macro.

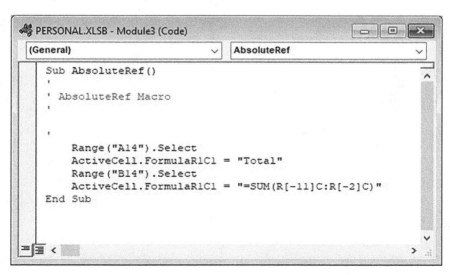

Notice that the macro is referring to specific cell addresses in lines 1 and 3 in the block of code. The macro selects cell **A14** and enters "Total". It then selects cell **B14** and enters the formula.

This means no matter where you try to run this macro on your worksheet, it will always enter the values in cells A14 and B14.

Relative Reference Macro

In this example, we're recording the same macro using relative references. *Relative reference* means relative to the cell that's currently active. So, you have to keep this in mind when you record and run the macro.

1. On the **Developer** tab, in the **Code** group, click **Use Relative References** to select it.

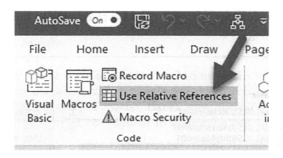

2. Next, click the **Record Macro** button on the **Developer** tab.

    This opens the **Record Macro** dialog box.

3. In the **Macro Name** field of the **Record Macro** dialog box, enter the name of the macro, for example, *RelativeRef*.

4. In the **Store macro in** drop-down list, select **Personal Macro Workbook** (if it's not already selected).

5. Click **OK** to start recording.

At this point, Excel is recording your actions. Carry out the following steps:

6. Select cell A14 and type **Total** in the cell.

7. Select cell B14 and type **=SUM(B3:B12)**.

8. On the **Developer** tab, click **Stop Recording** to stop recording the macro.

3. ASSIGN MACROS TO BUTTONS

On most occasions, for frequently used macros, we want a method of running the macro that is easy and straightforward. It could become a pain to open the Macro dialog box to find and run the right macro each time we want to run the macro. An easier way to do this is to create a command button on the ribbon that you can use to run the macro with one click. You can also assign the macro to objects you've inserted in your worksheet, like Form Control buttons, images, or icons.

In this chapter, we will cover how to:
- Create a custom tab and group on the Ribbon.
- Assign a macro button to your custom group.
- Assign a macro to a button on the Quick Access Toolbar.
- Assign a macro to a graphic object, for example, an image or an icon.
- Assign a macro to a Form Control button.

Add a Macro Button to the Ribbon

To assign a macro to a command button that you add to the Ribbon, you have to create a new custom group. This is because you cannot add the macro button to one of the default groups in Excel. You can create a new custom group in one of the default tabs and add your macro button there. Alternatively, you can create a new custom tab in which you add your new custom group and your macro command button.

Create a New Custom Tab and Group

The following steps go through the process of creating a new tab and then adding a command button to it.

1. To create a **new tab**, click the **New Tab** button at the bottom of the Main Tabs list box. Inside the tab, you must create at least one group before you can add a command button from the left side of the screen.

2. To give the tab a display name, select the **New Tab (Custom)** item and click the **Rename** button at the bottom of the Main Tabs list box. Enter your preferred name for the tab in the **Rename** dialog box and click **OK.**

3. You can use the arrow buttons to the right of the Main Tabs list box to move your new tab item up or down the list, depending on where you want to place it.

4. To create a new **custom group**, select the tab in which you want to create the group. This could be one of the default tabs, for example, **Home**, or the new one you've created. Click on the **New Group** button (at the bottom of the screen, under the Main Tabs list box). This will create a new group within the currently selected tab.

5. To create a display name for the group, select the **New Group (Custom)** item and click the **Rename** button. Enter your preferred name, for example, *MyMacros* in the **Rename** dialog box and click **OK.**

You now have a custom group in which you can add your macro command buttons.

Assign a Macro command to the new group

Follow the steps below to add a macro command button to the new custom group:

1. Select your custom group in the **Main Tabs** list box.

2. Click the drop-down list box named **Choose commands from** (on the left of the dialog box) and select **Macros** from the drop-down list. In the list box on the left, you'll see a list of macros created in the current workbook and saved in the PERSONAL.XLSB workbook.

3. Select the macro name that you want to add to your custom group in the list box on the left, then click the **Add** button to add the macro command to the new custom group in the list box on the right.

    Note: If you mistakenly added the wrong command, you can select it in the list box on the right and click the **Remove** button to remove it.

4. Click **OK** on the Excel Options dialog box to confirm the change.

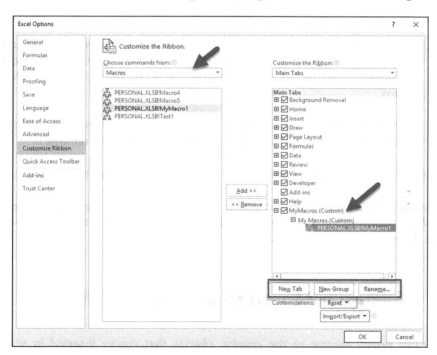

Assign a Macro to a Form Control Button

You can add an Excel **Form Control** from the Developer tab in your worksheet which you can use to execute macros. The **Button Form Control** is like a button on a form to which you can assign a macro. When you click the button, the macro runs in the current worksheet.

To add a button form control to your worksheet, do the following:

1. On the **Developer** tab, in the **Controls** group, click the **Insert** button, and then click the **Button (Form Control)** icon (topmost left on the drop-down menu).

2. In the body of the worksheet, draw the button with your mouse.

3. As soon as you release the left mouse button, the **Assign Macro** dialog box will open. Select the macro you want to assign to the button from the Macro name box and click **OK**.

4. Next, to edit the button's caption, right-click the button and select **Edit Text** from the pop-up menu then type the caption you want for the button.

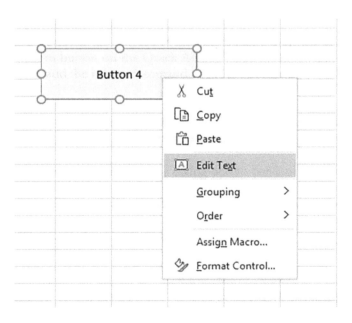

5. Click anywhere in the worksheet to exit the design mode. This will remove the selection from the button.

6. Your button is now set and ready for use. Whenever you click on the button, the macro you assigned to it will run in the current worksheet.

Notes:

- When you right-click the button to select it, it goes into design mode. To reactivate the button, click anywhere else in the worksheet. This removes the selection and the button will respond to clicks.

- To format the button and change other properties, for example, the font or caption, right-click the button and select **Format Control** from the pop-up menu. This will open the **Format Control** dialog box where you can change several properties of the control. When you're finished, click **OK** on the Format Control dialog box. Then, click any cell in your worksheet to remove the button from design mode.

4. MACRO SECURITY

As you're probably aware, Excel macros can be used to create viruses and other malicious code that can cause damage to a computer. Over the years, Microsoft has increasingly added security features in Excel to mitigate these threats. Managing security is a very important aspect of Excel macros. To create and use Excel macros, you need to know how to configure macro security, especially in a shared environment like a company network.

In this chapter, we will cover:
- What Trusted Documents are.
- The difference between macro-enabled workbooks and standard workbooks.
- How to configure your Trust Center settings for your macro needs.
- How to configure trusted locations, especially if you are in an office environment.

Trusted Documents

Excel 2019 uses an authentication system called Microsoft Authenticode to digitally sign macro projects or add-ins created with VBA. The macros you create locally on your computer are automatically authenticated so when you run them on your computer, Excel does not display a security alert.

For macros from an external source, the developer can acquire a certificate issued by a reputable authority or a trusted publisher. In such cases, Excel will run the macro if it can verify that it is from a trusted source.

If Excel cannot verify the digital signature of a macro from an external source, because it perhaps doesn't have one, a security alert is displayed in the message bar (below the Excel Ribbon). This alert gives you the option to enable or ignore the macro.

If you trust the source and you're sure that the file poses no security threat to your computer, you can click the **Enable Content** button to enable macros in the workbook. If you click Enable Content once, that file automatically becomes a trusted document on your computer. This ensures you don't keep receiving the security prompt each time you open the file, which could be a real nuisance for a file you've already indicated that you trusted.

Macro-enabled Workbooks

You cannot save macros in a normal Excel file with an XLSX extension. This ensures that you can be sure that an Excel file is safe from malicious code if it has a standard extension. On the other hand, if a file is macro-enabled (has an XLSM or XLSB extension), you'll be aware of the potential risk it poses and will only click 'enable macros' if the file is from a trusted location.

If you create a macro in an Excel workbook and try to save it with an XLSX extension, Excel will display a message informing you that macros cannot be saved in the file and that you must save it as a macro-enabled workbook.

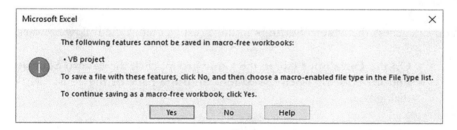

If you choose to continue saving it, the macro will be stripped off.

To save the macro in the file you need to select the **Excel Macro-Enabled Workbook (*.xlsm)** file extension from the filter list in the **Save As** screen.

The Personal Macro Workbook

At the time of creating the macro, you can choose to save it to your **Personal Macro Workbook**. When you do this, it will be saved in the PERSONAL.XLSB file, which is an Excel Binary Workbook in the XLSTART folder. In this case, you'll not need to save your workbook as a macro-enabled workbook.

When creating a macro for use on your computer, as much as possible, you want to store the macro in the Personal Macro Workbook. This means the macro will be global on your computer and can be run from any Excel workbook on your computer. It also means that you don't need to convert multiple workbooks into macro-enabled files. Only use an individual macro-enabled workbook if there is a specific reason to do so, for example, you want to distribute the file to other people.

Trust Center Macro Settings

Microsoft Office security and privacy settings are located in the **Trust Center**. The Macro Settings tab of the Trust Center contains the macro security settings for your computer. Macro security is important to protect your computer against the threat of malicious code that can be inserted in Microsoft Office macros.

You can access the **Macro Settings** in the Trust Center in the following ways:

- On the **Developer** tab, in the **Code** group, click the **Macro Security** button. This will open the **Macro Settings** pane of the Trust Center dialog box.

- On the Ribbon, click the **File** tab and then click **Options** > **Trust Center** > **Trust Centre Settings** > **Macro Settings**.

By default, Excel 2019 disables all macros from external sources with a security alert on the message bar, giving you the option to enable the macro or ignore it. This is the default setting when you install Excel, but there are other security options from which you can choose.

You can also select one of these options in Macro Settings:

- **Disable all macros without notification**: This automatically disables macros in your computer. This setting means no macros will run on your computer and you'll not get a security alert giving you the option to run the macro. This option is useful for shared computers, for example, where you don't want anyone using the computer to run macros.

- **Disable all macros with notification**: This option is the default. All macros from external sources are disabled with a security alert showing on the message bar. With this option, you have to specifically choose to enable the macro before it can run.

- **Disable all macros except digitally signed macros**: This option disables all macros apart from the digitally signed macros from publishers that you have added to your **Trusted Publishers** in the Trust Center. When you have this option selected and you get a macro from a publisher that's not in your Trusted Publishers list, you will get an alert in the message bar with a **Trust All Documents from this Publisher** button that you can click to add them to your trusted publishers.

- **Enable all macros (not recommended; potentially dangerous code can run)**: This option enables all macros without any notifications or security alerts, even for the macros that are not digitally signed or authenticated. As stated in its label, this option is not recommended because you can inadvertently run malicious code that corrupts your data or damages your computer.

Trusted Locations

The **Trusted Locations** tab of the Trust Center dialog box enables you to add, remove or modify trusted locations. If you are receiving macros from an external source that you need to run on your computer without alerts, then you need to place them in a trusted location on your computer. In doing so, Excel knows that these files are safe, and you are not prompted with security alerts when you open them.

You can use the following options to change Trusted Locations settings:

- **Add new location**: To add a new trusted location, click the **Add new location** button at the bottom of the screen. On the **Microsoft Office Trusted Location** dialog box, click on the **Browse** button and navigate to the folder that you want to add to the list of trusted locations. After selecting the folder, click **OK** on the Browse dialog box, and **OK** again on the **Microsoft Office Trusted Location** dialog box to confirm the entry.

   This will add in a new trusted location on your computer and you can store any externally created macro-enabled files in that folder.

- **Allow trusted locations on my network (not recommended):** Click this option if you want to add folders on your network to your trusted locations. As indicated by the label, this is not recommended by Microsoft as you cannot entirely trust the safety of external locations. However, if you're working on a shared network drive that you trust, and that is the only way you can collaborate with others, then this may be an option for sharing macro-enabled files. Only use as a last option.

- **Disable all trusted locations**: Check this box if you want to immediately disable all trusted locations. This means macros in these locations would not run and only the macros that are digitally signed and recognised as trustworthy by Excel will run on your computer.

Note: The macro-enabled worksheets you create locally on your computer do not need to be stored in a trusted location to run on your computer. This is because they're automatically digitally authenticated by Excel.

5. VISUAL BASIC FOR APPLICATIONS ESSENTIALS

Visual Basic for Applications (VBA for short) is a vast subject area. Our focus here will be on aspects of the language that can be of immediate use to you in terms of editing your recorded macros, creating new small procedures, and creating user-defined functions.

In this chapter, we will cover:

- Variables at how to declare them.
- Properties and how to use them.
- How to insert new modules.
- The difference between Sub procedures and Function procedures and how to insert them in your project.
- Essential VBA constructs for decision making and controlling program flow.

VBA and Macros

There are three ways you can create a macro in Excel:

1. Record your actions with the macro recorder.

2. Directly write the code in the code editor.

3. The third method is a hybrid of the first two. You first use the macro recorder to record your actions in Excel and let the recorder generate the source code for you. Then you edit the source code to put in the finishing touches.

As a beginner in Excel VBA, the third method is how you should start creating your macros. Even veteran VBA developers use this method to expedite the process. You often only need to write macros from scratch if you're creating new instances of objects and manipulating them in code.

The Visual Basic Editor Overview

The Visual Basic Editor is an application built into Excel with its own menu and command buttons. You can't run the Visual Basic Editor as a separate application, you can only open it from within Excel.

To open the Visual Basic Editor, click the **Developer** tab, and in the **Code** group, click on the **Visual Basic** command button.

Tip: A quick way to activate the Visual Basic Editor is to press Alt+F11 when Excel is active. You can also press Alt+F11 to return to Excel when you are done with the Visual Basic Editor, or you can simply click the **Close** button on the Visual Basic Editor toolbar.

The image below shows the Visual Basic Editor and some of the key parts which are identified. At first glance, the Visual Basic Editor may look quite busy, but it becomes familiar very quickly when you spend some time using it. The Visual Basic Editor is made up of several windows that are highly customisable. You can rearrange, hide, or dock windows in different parts of the screen. The two most important windows, when you're first starting to use the Visual Basic Editor, are the Project window (or Project Explorer) and the Code window.

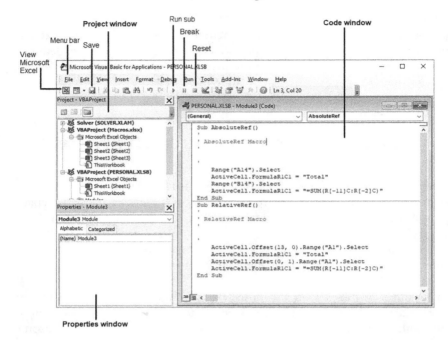

Menu bar

The menu bar for the Visual Basic Editor works just like the menu bar of other applications you've encountered. It contains commands that you can use to carry out various tasks within the editor. Many of the menu commands also have shortcut keys for them.

Toolbar

Under the menu bar, you have one or more toolbars. These have several command buttons that make it easy to access many of the commands with one click. You can customise the toolbars by adding more commands, move them around, or display other toolbars. The standard toolbar would be sufficient for most new users of the Visual Basic Editor.

Project window

The Project window displays a collapsible tree that shows all the workbooks currently open in Excel and the code modules associated with them. You can double-click items on the list to expand or contract them. If you can't see the Project window, press **Ctrl+Alt**, or click **View >Project Explorer** on the menu bar to display the window. You can hide the Project window by clicking the close button in its title bar, or right-click anywhere in the Project window and select **Hide** from the pop-up menu.

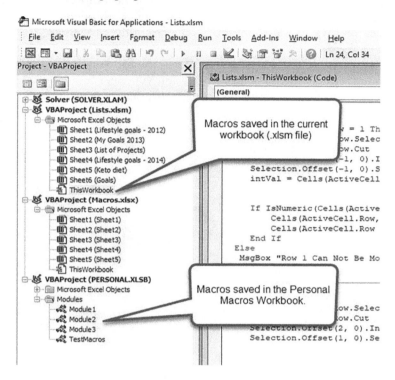

Note that a 'project' is made up of all the code and other objects that belong to a particular workbook like worksheets and form controls.

Code window

The code window contains the VBA code recorded with a macro or directly inserted manually. Every object displayed in the Project window has an associated code window. To view the code window for an object in the Project window, double-click on the object. For example, to display the code window for Sheet1, double-click Sheet1 in the Project window and the code window for sheet one will be displayed on the right. If you haven't added any code the code window will be empty.

The macros that you create are stored in modules which are given names like Module1, Module2, Module3 and so on. You can view them in the code window by double-clicking on the module name in the Project Explorer window.

Properties window

The properties window allows you to rename a module. For example, you may want to give a more descriptive name to Module1 or Module2. To do this, simply click on the module you want to rename. In the properties window, in the name field, enter a descriptive name and press enter. When you rename the module, you must use the same naming convention for worksheet ranges. That is, you must begin the name with a letter, and you can't insert spaces in the name. If you want to separate two words, use an underscore instead, for example, *Totals_2019*.

Using Variables

You can imagine a variable as a named memory location in which you can temporarily hold data. Once created, you can then use the name to refer to that memory location for the rest of the procedure. You can store data, update data, and retrieve data from the variable as your program runs.

Variable Data Types

There are different types of variables for the different datatypes they hold. Some of the common variable types in VBA are:

- **String**: Holds text data.

- **Integer**: Holds integer numbers ranging from −32,768 to 32,767

- **Long**: Holds integer numbers ranging from −2,147,483,648 to 2,147,483,647

- **Double**: Holds floating-point numbers, for example, 5.5, 0.01, and -2,345.6789

- **Variant**: Holds any kind of data.

- **Boolean**: Holds True or False.

- **Object**: Holds an object from the Excel object model.

Variable Naming Conventions

There are certain naming rules you must follow for variables.

- The first character must be a letter.

- Only use alphabetic or numeric characters.

- Do not name your variables the same names within the same scope.

- Do not use spaces in your variable names. Use a combination of uppercase and lowercase characters, or an underscore, to separate two words.

- Variable names cannot be more than 255 characters. Of course, you would not want to make your variable name anywhere near that long.

To make your code easier to read and maintain, one recommendation is to add a three-letter prefix of the datatype to the variable name. For example, *strCustomerName* indicates that the variable is of a string datatype. This is just a recommendation, of course. What's more important is to use a name that describes the variable.

You can use a combination of uppercase and lowercase characters to separate two words in your variable name or you can use an underscore. For instance, use *strCustomerName* instead of *strcustomername*.

After declaring a variable, with subsequent use in your procedure, VBA's automatic syntax checking will convert it to its proper case (that is the case in which it was declared). This helps you to quickly determine if you've mistyped a variable name. If the automatic syntax checking feature does not correct the case of a variable name you typed in all lowercase, then you know it was mistyped. Mistyped variables can lead to bugs and errors that are very difficult to find if Option Explicit is not enabled.

Declaring Variables

To explicitly declare a variable in a procedure, you have to use the **Dim** keyword (which is an abbreviation for Dimension), followed by the name of your variable, and then the datatype.

For example:

```
Dim txtHeading As String
Dim intMyNumber As Integer
Dim varText As Variant
```

After you declare a variable, you assign a value to it by using the equal sign operator.

Assigning Values to Variables

To assign a value to a variable you need to use an assignment statement. An assignment statement assigns the value or result of an expression to a variable or an object.

If you've created formulas in Excel before then you'll be familiar with the concept of expressions. In Excel, to insert a formula in a cell, you precede the formula with an equal sign (=). In VBA, you use the equal sign to assign values to variables.

Below are examples of how you assign a value to a variable:

```
txtMyText = "Figures for 2010 To 2019"
```

This statement assigns the text "Figures for 2010 To 2019" to an area in memory named txtHeading. Once assigned, you can now use this variable name to refer to that piece of text in memory for the rest of the procedure.

```
intMyNumber = Range("A1").Value
```

This statement assigns the value in cell A1 in the current worksheet to intMyNumber. Once assigned, you can then use this variable name to refer to that number in memory for the rest of the procedure.

You can also assign the result of an expression to a variable, for example:

```
Sum = num1 + num2
```

In this case, the values in two variables are added up and the sum is passed to a third variable called Sum.

Unlike mathematical calculations where the answer ends up on the right of the statement, in programming, an assignment goes from right to left. Hence the answer of an evaluation will end up in the leftmost variable before the equal sign. Just remember that the equal sign has two roles in VBA. It can be used as an assignment operator as well as a comparison operator.

Examples of variable declaration, assignment, and then use:

```
Sub Assignment()
    'Declare variables
    Dim intCOunt As Integer
    Dim varRate As Variant
    Dim dblAmount As Double
    Dim bolStatus As Boolean
    Dim strUserName As String
    Dim datStartDate As Date

    'Assign values to the variables
    intCOunt = 0
    intCOunt = intCOunt + 1
    varRate = 0.025
    dblAmount = 34382.67
    bolStatus = False
    strUserName = "Bob Johnson"
    datStartDate = #1/1/2020#

    'Display the values in a message box
    MsgBox intCOunt & vbNewLine & _
        varRate & vbNewLine & _
        dblAmount & vbNewLine & _
        bolStatus & vbNewLine & _
        strUserName & vbNewLine & _
        datStartDate
End Sub
```

Using Option Explicit

VBA allows you to use undeclared variables, meaning you can just create a name anywhere in your procedure and assign a value to it. For small lines of code, quick mock-ups, or demo code, where maintenance will not be an issue, it is OK to use undeclared variables.

However, for any kind of substantial work or work done in a production environment, it is highly recommended that you always declare your variables at the beginning of the procedure. This makes the code easier to maintain as you can see all local variables used at the top of each procedure.

A step you can take to ensure that all variables used in your module are explicitly declared is to add the statement **Option Explicit** at the top of the module.

```
Option Explicit
```

This will force the issue of declaring variables before use, otherwise, VBA generates a syntax error.

You can go a step further and enable the **Require Variable Declaration** option under **Code Settings** in the Visual Basic Editor Options dialog box.

To enforce variable declaration for all new modules, do the following:

1. On the Visual Basic Editor toolbar, click **Tools > Options** to open the **Options** dialog box.

2. On the **Editor** tab of the Options dialog box, select the **Require Variable Declaration** checkbox.

3. Click **OK**.

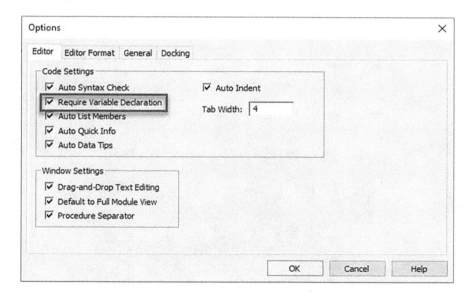

When you enable this option, all new modules created will automatically have the Option Explicit statement inserted at the top of the module.

Tip: Use the Option Explicit statement in your modules to prevent errors caused by mistyped variable names. If Option Explicit is not present, you can just type any variable name and use it at any point in your code. This may make writing the code a little faster, but a major downside is that it can introduce errors in your code that are very difficult to spot.

You can mistype a variable name you've used in other parts of your program, but VBA's automatic syntax checking feature will not flag this as an error. The mistyped variable name may lead to inconsistent results when you run your code, but as far as VBA is concerned the code is valid. If you want to avoid this kind of error altogether, always put Option Explicit at the top of your modules.

Note: As the code examples used in this book are for demonstration purposes only, for brevity, the variables used may not always be explicitly declared.

Operators in VBA

The operators in VBA work in a similar way to Excel operators. So, if you're familiar with Excel operators, the operators in VBA will be second nature to you. The one slight difference is the modulus operator. To carry out mod calculations in Excel, you use the MOD function. In VBA, you use the Mod operator just like any of the other operators.

Arithmetic Operators

The following arithmetic operators are used to perform basic mathematical calculations in VBA such as addition, subtraction, multiplication, or division.

Arithmetic operator	Meaning
* (asterisk)	Multiplication
^ (caret)	Exponentiation
/ (forward slash)	Normal division
\ (backslash)	Divide two numbers and return an integer result.
Mod (modulus)	Divide two numbers and return only the remainder.
+ (plus sign)	Addition
– (minus sign)	Subtraction or Negation

Comparison Operators

Comparison operators allow you to compare two values and return a logical value, that is, TRUE or FALSE.

Comparison operator	Meaning
=	Equal to
>	Greater than
<	Less than
>=	Greater than or equal to
<=	Less than or equal to
<>	Not equal to

Concatenation

Concatenation operator	Meaning
& (ampersand)	Used to combine two expressions.

Logical Operators

Logical operator	Meaning
And	Returns TRUE if both expressions are true, otherwise, it returns FALSE.
Or	Returns TRUE if any part is true, otherwise, it returns FALSE.
Not	Performs a logical negation on an expression. That is, it reverses true and false. For example, 'Not A=B' returns TRUE if A=B is false and returns FALSE if A=B is true.

Note: There are other logical operators in VBA, but these three are the only ones you're ever likely to use in your VBA programming career.

Operator Precedence

If you combine several operators in a single statement, VBA performs the operations in the following order:

Order	Arithmetic operator	Meaning
1	^	Exponentiation
2	-	Negation
3	*, /	Multiplication and floating-point division
4	\	Integer division
5	Mod	Modulus arithmetic
6	+, -	Addition and subtraction
7	&	String concatenation

- **Function procedure**: A function procedure is a set of programming instructions that performs a calculation and returns a single value (similar to a worksheet function in excel like SUM). Functions have to be coded manually.

A module can be used to store one type of code or a mix of all three. The type of code you use depends on the functionality you're looking to create. You can also use different modules to store procedures for the same project, for example, as a way to organise them for easier maintenance. How you choose to arrange your code is down to personal preference.

How to Insert a New Module

To insert a new module, carry out the following steps:

1. Select the project's name in the Project window.

2. On the Visual Basic Editor menu bar, click **Insert** and select **Module** from the menu (alternatively, you can right-click the project's name and choose **Insert** > **Module** from the shortcut menu).

A new module will be added to the Modules folder under the selected Project.

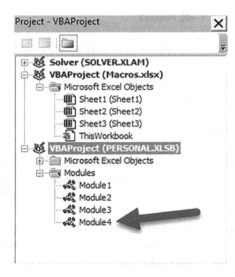

There may be occasions when you want to remove a module, for example, if you created it by mistake or if it's no longer needed.

To remove a module, follow these steps:

1. Select the module's name in the Project window.

2. On the Visual Basic Editor menu bar, click **File**, and select Remove [module name] from the menu. Alternatively, you can right-click the module name and select Remove [module name] from the shortcut menu.

3. Excel will prompt you with a message asking if you want to export the code in the module before you delete it. Click the **No** button if you want to go ahead with the deletion.

   Note: If you want to keep a copy of the code before removing the module, click the **Yes** button. Excel will display a dialog box, enabling you to save the code in a text file with a Basic File (.bas) extension.

To rename a module, do the following:

1. In the Project window, select the module you want to rename.

2. In the Properties window, in the **Name** field, enter a new name for the module (overwriting the old name) and press enter. The name must start with a letter and cannot have spaces. If you want to separate two words, you can use an underscore or capitalization.

Note: It's not always necessary to rename modules from the default name given by the Visual Basic Editor. The name you give your procedure is what counts when it comes to executing a macro or a piece of code entered manually. However, if you have lots of modules in one project, you may want to name them as a way to organise your code, which would make it easier to maintain.

Procedures

When you record a macro, the set of VBA code instructions that the macro recorder generates is known as a procedure. You can also create procedures manually by entering the code directly in the Visual Basic Editor. There are two types of procedures, **Sub** procedures and **Function** procedures.

Sub Procedures

A Sub procedure is a set of programming instructions that, when executed, performs a series of actions in Excel. A Sub procedure starts with the **Sub** keyword and ends with the **End Sub** statement. The macro recorder always creates a Sub procedure that takes no arguments.

```
Sub AddNumbers()
   Sum = 1 + 2
   MsgBox "The sum is " & Sum
End Sub
```

The Sub procedure example above sums up two numbers and displays the sum to the user in a message box.

A Sub procedure can have zero or more arguments that you pass in when you call the Sub procedure from another procedure. If your Sub has one or more arguments, list them between the parentheses. For example:

```
Sub AddNumbers(num1, num2)
   Sum = num1 + num2
   MsgBox "The sum is " & Sum
End Sub
```

In the example above, the Sub procedure has two arguments which are used inside the procedure to calculate the sum.

Function Procedures

A Function procedure is a set of programming instructions that carries out an evaluation (or a series of evaluations) and returns a single value (for example, the way Excel functions like SUM, COUNT, LEN work). Just like some built-in Excel functions, some advanced Function procedures can also be written to return a series of values in an array. You can specify the data type that the Function procedure returns. For instance, you can declare a function to return a text string, date, or currency.

A Function procedure starts with the **Function** keyword and ends with an **End Function** statement. Function procedures cannot be created with the macro recorder so have to be created manually.

Example:

```
Function MyTotal(num1, num2)
   MyTotal = num1 * num2
End Function
```

This function takes in two numbers as arguments and returns their product. After the work in the function is done, you assign the value to be returned to the function name, telling VBA to return the value and exit the function.

Procedure Naming Conventions

The naming convention for procedures is very similar to that of variables:

- The first character must be a letter.

- You can only use alphanumeric characters. You can't use characters like @, &, #, !, $, ^, *, or %.

- You can't use spaces between procedure names. You can separate two words with an underscore or capitalisation.

- The procedure name cannot be more than 255 characters (but you certainly don't want to use anywhere near that length).

- Ideally, you want the procedure name to describe its purpose. One method you can use is to combine a verb and a noun, for example, AddData, PrintValues, CalculateTotal, or SortData.

How to Insert Procedures

You can enter new Sub procedures and Function procedures manually in the Visual Basic Editor's code window. To enter a piece of code from scratch in the Visual Basic Editor, follow these general steps:

1. **Insert a new module in the chosen project.**

   If you want to write a macro for the current workbook, click the name of the project in Project Explorer for the current workbook. This should have the name of the workbook in parenthesis after the label VBAProject, for example, **VBAProject (MyWorksheetName)**. If you want to place the macro in the Personal Macro Workbook, select **VBAProject (PERSONAL.XLSB)**.

   Insert a module in the selected project by following the steps detailed for how to insert a new module covered in the Modules section earlier in this book.

   Once you've inserted the new module, double-click the module name to open it in the code window on the right pane.

2. **Enter the start and end statements for the procedure.**

   Start a Sub procedure with the **Sub** keyword followed by a space and then the name of the procedure, for example, **Sub myMacro** (for a Function procedure, use the **Function** keyword in place of Sub).

   When you press Enter, VBA will automatically enter the end statement (**End Sub** for a Sub procedure and **End Function** for a Function procedure)

3. Enter comments to document the procedure.

Before you begin writing your code in your procedure, you may want to include a brief description of what the procedure does, the date it was created, and your name (if you're working in a shared environment). This helps immensely with maintenance and should be standard practice in any production environment.

To add comments in your code, type an apostrophe at the beginning of each line of text you want to enter as a comment. VBA will ignore these lines and not execute them as code. With the default settings of the Visual Basic Editor, comments are identified in the code window as green text. This enables you to tell the difference between comments and executable code.

Note: You can also use an apostrophe to comment out code that you don't want to run. For example, you may want to test how your code works without a particular statement, instead of deleting it, you can add an apostrophe in front of it like this:

```
'Selection.Columns.AutoFit
```

4. Write your code.

When you write your code. You can make it more legible with indentation. You can press **Tab** to indent a line of code if you want it to appear within another block of code. To outdent a line of code, place the insertion point before the first character and hit the backspace key, or select the line and press **Shift + Tab**.

To indent a block of code, select all the required lines and press **Tab**. To outdent a selected block of code, press the **Shift + Tab** keys.

5. Save your procedure.

Once you are done, you can save your macro by clicking **File > Save** on the menu bar. Alternatively, you can click on the blue disk icon on the toolbar to save your work.

6. Test your code.

Run your code to ensure it does what it is supposed to do. How you run your code will depend on what type of procedure you've created.

See the next section for the different ways you can execute Sub procedures and Function procedures.

How to Execute a Sub Procedure

Once you've created a Sub procedure, you can run it in a variety of ways. We have already touched on some of them in previous chapters on how to run a macro.

You can run a Sub procedure in the following ways:

- From Excel's Macro dialog box.

- Assign it as a macro to a custom button on the Excel Ribbon.

- Assign it as a macro to a command button on the Quick Access Toolbar.

- Assign it to a Form button or graphic object in your worksheet.

- Run it from the Visual Basic Editor using the Run Sub/UserForm command.

- Call it from another procedure.

The first four methods in the list above have been covered previously in this book (in chapters 1 and 3), so we'll focus on the last two methods here.

Run a Procedure in The Visual Basic Editor

You can run a Sub procedure directly from the Visual Basic Editor (if it has no arguments). This is a method often used during debugging or when you're experimenting with some statements and you want to quickly see the results.

To run a Sub procedure from the Visual Basic Editor, do the following:

1. Place the cursor in the Sub procedure you want to run.

2. On the Visual Basic Editor toolbar, select **Run** > **Run Sub/UserForm**.

—or—

Press the F5 key.

—or—

Click the **Run Sub/UserForm** icon on the toolbar (the green right-pointing triangle icon on the toolbar).

Call a Sub Procedure from Another Procedure

You can call a Sub procedure from inside another Sub procedure or a Function procedure. If you have a large application, one way to organise your code is to have a main Sub procedure from which other Sub or Function procedures, that contain the details, are called. This makes it easier to read the code as you're grouping related actions into different procedures.

To call a Sub procedure from another procedure, type the name of the procedure, including any required arguments. The **Call** keyword is required if your Sub procedure has arguments and they're enclosed in parentheses when called. Using Call is optional for all other cases.

In the example below, a Sub procedure is called from within another Sub procedure named *Main*. *CarPrice* has no arguments while *CarCalc* has two arguments. CarCalc has been called using two different methods in the Main Sub.

> In the first executable statement in the Main Sub, CarPrice was called and it has no parameters.

> In the second executable statement in Main, CarCalc was called without parentheses around the arguments, hence we didn't have to use the Call keyword.

> In the third executable statement in Main, CarCalc was called with parentheses around the arguments, in this case, the Call keyword needed to be used.

```
Sub Main()
    ' call a Sub without arguments
    CarPrice

    ' call a Sub with 2 arguments
    CarCalc 20800, 30100

    'call a Sub with 2 arguments enclosed parentheses
    Call CarCalc(25950, 49500)
End Sub

Sub CarPrice()
    MsgBox "The car price is: " & "$20,800"
End Sub

Sub CarCalc(price, income)
    If (income / 12) * 0.2 <= (price * 1.025) / 36 Then
        MsgBox "You cannot afford this car."
    Else
        MsgBox "This car is affordable."
    End If
End Sub
```

Executing Function Procedures

Unlike Sub procedures, Function procedures can only be executed in two ways:

- You can call the function from another Sub procedure or Function procedure.

- You can use a function directly in your worksheet just as you use a built-in Excel function.

Calling a function from another procedure

As a function returns a value, you have to incorporate the function call in a statement that assigns the return value to a variable in your procedure. Functions are usually called in procedures to process a request or to perform an evaluation. The result is then passed to the calling procedure where the value is then used.

In the example below, we have a Sub procedure named Main in which a function named *MonthlyInterest* is called. MonthlyInterest takes in two arguments, *Capital* and *Rate*, and returns the monthly interest on the capital.

In our main procedure, we want to calculate the monthly interest on an investment of $100,000 at an annual interest rate of 2.5%.

All we need to do in the main procedure is, call the MonthlyInterest function and pass in the values we want to calculate as its arguments. The statement returns the result to our local variable called *myInterest*. The value returned is then displayed in a message box to the user.

```
Sub Main()
    Dim myInterest As Currency
    myInterest = MonthlyInterest(100000, 0.025)
    MsgBox "The monthly interest is: $" & myInterest
End Sub

Function MonthlyInterest(Capital, Rate)
    MonthlyInterest = (Capital * Rate) / 12
End Function
```

Calling a function from your worksheet as a formula

When you create Sub procedures, they become available in Excel as macros. On the other hand, when you create Function procedures, they become available in Excel as user-defined functions. You can use these functions in Excel just like any of the other built-in Excel functions. Any Function procedure you create in Excel will be available in the **User Defined** category in the **Insert Functions** dialog box.

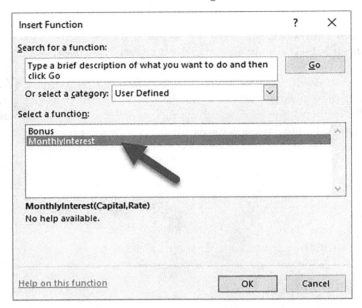

For a detailed tutorial on how to create and use user-defined functions in your Excel worksheets, see chapter 9.

Program Flow

To create custom functions in VBA that carry out specific calculations you'll need to be familiar with some of the Visual Basic constructs for decision making. If you've used conditional or logical functions like the IF function in Excel before, then you would be familiar with the concept of these constructs.

If... Then... Else

If you have used the IF function in Excel, then you would be familiar with how a conditional statement works. **If... then... Else** enables you to create a conditional statement that executes the enclosed code when a condition is met.

At a basic level, this code says:

"If this is true, then do this…"

An **If** statement does not necessarily need to have an **Else** part. The Else part is only required if you have another statement to execute in the event of the first one failing the test.

In the example below, we're testing whether the value in varSpend is greater than $10,000. If it evaluates to TRUE, the next line of code is executed, and the program exits the If block. If the test evaluates to FALSE, then the program skips to the **Else** block and executes the statement(s) there before exiting the If block.

```
If varSpend > 10000 Then
   txtReturn = "Over Budget"
Else
   txtReturn = "Within Budget"
End If
```

Select Case

Select Case is another Visual Basic construct that you may use when creating user-defined functions. The closest Excel function to **Select Case** is the SWITCH function, which was covered in detail in my Excel 2019 Functions book.

Select Case enables you to choose one of several 'cases' based on the value of one expression. This can also be performed by building complex **If... Then... Else** statements, but Select Case is usually more efficient because the test expression is evaluated only once.

In the example below, the value in *score* is evaluated once and compared with multiple **Case** statements. The code under the Case statement that passes the test is executed before the program exits the Select Case block. You can use a **Case Else** statement to catch anything else not matched in the other Case statement.

```
Select Case score
    Case Is >= 70
        result = "Merit"
    Case Is >= 50
        result = "Credit"
    Case Is >= 40
        result = "Pass"
    Case Else
        result = "Fail"
End Select
```

These two constructs should cover any scenario where you would use a conditional statement.

Do...Loop

If you want to create procedures based on more complex decisions, you can use a looping construct like the **Do...Loop**. A **Do...Loop** statement repeats a block of code *while* the condition being tested is true, or *until* the condition being tested is true.

There are two types of **Do** loops. Use **Do...While** to repeat a section of code *while* a condition remains true and use **Do...Until** to repeat a section of code *until* a condition becomes true.

At a basic level, it says:

Repeat this block of code [while/until] the condition being tested is true.

You can place the test (or condition) at the top of the loop or at the bottom of the loop, depending on your specific scenario.

Syntax

You can place the test at the top of the loop:

    Do [{ While | Until } condition]
      [statements]
    [Exit Do]
      [statements]
    Loop

Or, place the test at the bottom of the loop:

    Do
      [statements]
    [Exit Do]
      [statements]
    Loop [{ While | Until } condition]

In the example below, the **Do...While** loop continues to run the enclosed code while the user enters a number in the input box.

With each iteration, the Do...While loop checks that the value in **varInput** is not empty (marked with the empty quotes) and uses the result of this test to either run the segment of code again or exit the loop.

```
Sub NumberEntry()
    ' Do Loop example using the InputBox to enter numbers

    Dim varInput As Variant
    Dim lngTotal As Long

    varInput = InputBox("Enter a number or press Cancel
to end")

    Do While varInput <> ""
        lngTotal = lngTotal + varInput
        varInput = InputBox("Enter a number in the text
box or press Cancel to finish")
    Loop

    MsgBox "The total is: " & lngTotal

End Sub
```

The program exits the loop when the user clicks the Cancel button on the input box meaning varInput will be empty.

You can place an **Exit Do** statement anywhere in the **Do…Loop** as an alternate way to exit the loop. **Exit Do** is optional, and only used to immediately exit the loop if a certain condition is met before the end of the loop.

In the example below the Do…Loop is set the loop while intCount is less than or equal to 100. However, within the loop we use an **If** statement to check the value of intCount and if it's greater than 10 then run the Exit Do statement to exit the loop.

```
Sub Increment()
    Dim intCount As Integer
    intCount = 0

    Do While intCount <= 100
        If intCount > 10 Then
            Exit Do    ' Exits loop if intCount>10
        End If
        MsgBox "The current value is: " & intCount
        intCount = intCount + 2
    Loop

End Sub
```

For...Next

This is one of the simpler VBA loops in that it is designed from the onset to loop a specified number of times. If you know how many times you want a section of code to run, you can create a **For...Next** statement that executes the code a specific number of times.

A counter variable keeps track of how many times the code has iterated. In the example below, lngCount is the counter variable and it has been assigned the number range of 1 to 100. This means it will run 100 times. With each loop, the number in lngCount is incremented by 1 until it gets to 100, at which point the loop ends.

```
Sub AddMyNums()

    ' For..Next loop to add numbers using a set number of
loops

    Dim lngCount As Long
    Dim lngTotal As Long

    lngTotal = 0

    For lngCount = 1 To 100
        lngTotal = lngTotal + lngCount
    Next lngCount

    MsgBox "The total is: " & lngTotal

End Sub
```

There are variations to the **For...Next**. For example, you can use the **Step** statement to change the rate at which the loop increments the counter.

Let's say we add **Step 2** to the previous example, the loop will skip every even number in the specified range (1 to 100), hence will only run 50 times.

```
For lngCount = 1 To 100 Step 2
    lngTotal = lngTotal + lngCount
Next lngCount
```

Just like how the Exit Do statement can be used in the Do...Loop, you can include one or more **Exit For** statements within a For...Next loop. **Exit For** is

MsgBox function arguments:

Argument	Description
prompt	Required. This is the text you want to display to the user in the message box. You can have a maximum of 1024 characters. If the text is long, you can break it into several lines with the vbNewLine constant that inserts a carriage return in the text string.
buttons	Optional. This is a number that specifies the number and type of buttons to display. If you omit this argument, the default will be 0, which is the OK button only.
title	Optional. This is the text that you want to show in the title bar of the dialog box. If you omit this argument, the application name will be displayed on the title bar.
helpfile	Optional. This text string identifies the Help file that provides context-sensitive Help for the dialog box. If this argument is used, then the context argument must also be provided. Unless you're providing context-sensitive help, this argument is not necessary.
context	Optional. This is a number representing the number assigned to the appropriate Help topic. If this argument is provided, then the helpfile argument must also be provided. Again, unless you're providing context-sensitive help, you don't need to worry about this argument.

VBA constants for the MsgBox buttons argument:

Constant	Value	Description
vbOKOnly	0	Displays the OK button only.
vbOKCancel	1	Displays the OK and Cancel buttons.
vbAbortRetryIgnore	2	Displays the Abort, Retry, and Ignore buttons.
vbYesNoCancel	3	Displays the Yes, No, and Cancel buttons.
vbYesNo	4	Displays the Yes and No buttons.
vbRetryCancel	5	Displays the Retry and Cancel buttons.
vbCritical	16	Displays the Critical Message icon.
vbQuestion	32	Displays the Warning Query icon.
vbExclamation	48	Displays the Warning Message icon.
vbInformation	64	Displays the Information Message icon.
vbDefaultButton1	0	The first button is default.
vbDefaultButton2	256	The second button is default.
vbDefaultButton3	512	The third button is default.
vbDefaultButton4	768	The fourth button is default.

Notes:

- Use the constants with values 1-5 to specify the number and type of buttons to display in the message box.

- Use the constants with values 16, 32, 48, 64 to specify the type of icon to display in the message box.

- Use the constants with values 0, 256, 512, 768 to specify the default button. This is the button that has the focus by default when the message box is displayed.

VBA constants for the MsgBox return value:

Constant	Value	Description
vbOK	1	The user clicked OK.
vbCancel	2	The user clicked Cancel.
vbAbort	3	The user clicked Abort.
vbRetry	4	The user clicked Retry.
vbIgnore	5	The user clicked Ignore.
vbYes	6	The user clicked Yes.
vbNo	7	The user clicked No.

The return value is the value returned when the user clicks a button on the message box. There are also VBA constants for the return values. For example, if the user clicked **Cancel** in the dialog box, instead of checking whether the return value is 2, you'll check whether the return value is **vbCancel**. Using associated words rather than numbers makes them easier to remember.

Displaying a Simple Message Box

If you don't need to work with the response from the user, then don't put parentheses around the arguments of the MsgBox function.

In the example below, we've entered the *Prompt* and *Title* arguments but omitted the *Button* argument. When you omit a positional argument, you must include the corresponding comma delimiter.

```
MsgBox "The process is now complete.", , "My application"
```

This code will display the following message box:

In the example below, a simple message box is used to display the sum to the user, and it doesn't return a result. As soon as the message is displayed, the code is paused until the user clicks OK.

```
Sub SumNumbers()
    Dim Sum As Integer
    Sum = 1 + 2
    MsgBox "The sum is: " & Sum
End Sub
```

The only argument used is *prompt*. The prompt has to be enclosed in quotes as it is a text string. In this example, the ampersand (&) is used to concatenate the text in quotes with a number variable to make up the prompt.

Getting a Response from The User

If you want to capture the user's response when they click a button, then you need to use parentheses around the MsgBox function arguments. If you display a message box that has more than just the OK button, then you would want to know what button the user clicked.

To determine the type of buttons and icon to display on the message box, use the constants for the *button* argument (listed above). To use more than one of these constants as an argument, add them up with the + operator. For example, to display a message box with Yes and No buttons and a critical icon, use the following combination:

```
vbYesNo + vbCritical + vbDefaultButton2
```

The example below displays a critical-error message in a dialog box with **Yes** and **No** buttons. The **No** button has been specified as the default response.

Note that, the values for the arguments were first assigned to variables before being used in the MsgBox function. This makes the code easier to read. The value returned by the MsgBox function depends on which button the user clicks.

Notice that the MsgBox function arguments are enclosed in parentheses this time, and the return value is assigned to a variable.

```
Sub ProcessConfirm()
    Dim txtPrompt, intButtons, txtTitle, _
    intResponse, txtMyText

    txtPrompt = "Excel identified an issue. Do you want
to carry on with the process anyway?"
    intButtons = vbYesNo + vbCritical + vbDefaultButton2

 txtTitle = "MsgBox Demo"

    ' Display message.
    intResponse    =    MsgBox(txtPrompt,    intButtons,
txtTitle)
    If intResponse = vbYes Then    ' User clicked Yes.
       txtMyText = "Yes"    ' Perform this action.
       MsgBox "Your answer was Yes"
    Else    ' User clicked No.
       txtMyText = "No"    ' Perform this action.
       MsgBox "Your answer was No"
    End If
End Sub
```

This is how the message box looks when executed.

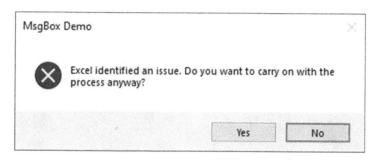

When the message is displayed, the code is paused until the user clicks **Yes** or **No**.

The line of code that follows then checks the value of the response. If the response is vbYes (meaning the user clicked the **Yes** button), the first part of the If statement is executed. If the response is not vbYes, the Else part of the If statement is executed (because it means the user selected **No**).

Tip: To capture a text input from the user at runtime using a message box, use the **InputBox** function. See chapter 8 for how to use the InputBox function.

6. DEBUGGING

In this chapter, we will cover the tools in the Visual Basic Editor that you can use to debug your code. Errors are something you'll encounter when writing code, even if you are an experienced programmer. Logic errors are especially difficult to find because syntactically, there is nothing wrong with the code, but it is just not producing the expected result. You'll use the debugging tools primarily for logic errors.

In this chapter, we will cover:
- An overview of debugging.
- Setting breakpoints in your code to enter break mode.
- Using the Immediate window to display information from your code.
- Using the Locals window to monitor variables and properties.
- How to use the Watch window to watch expressions.
- Using the Call Stack to trace the flow of code through multiple nested procedures.

Overview of Debugging

A game-changer for me in my early programming career was when I learned how to step through my code in break mode, observe the flow of the program, and what was happening to my variables. If there is one thing you take from this chapter, it should be how to step through your code in break mode and examine what variables are changing and what actions are changing them. This will save you a lot of time in trying to figure out why a procedure is not producing the expected results.

There are generally three types of errors in programming:

Syntax errors

Syntax errors occur when a mistake is made in the syntax. Examples include a keyword entered incorrectly, or a construct being used incorrectly, like using an **If** statement without an **End If**. Syntax errors are the easiest to identify as you won't even be able to run the code until you correct them.

The Visual Basic Editor has an automatic syntax checking feature (named **Auto Syntax Check** in the Visual Basic Editor options) that can detect and correct some syntax errors as you type your code. Those types of syntax errors generate an error message as soon as you try to leave the line, telling you what the error is and offering some help. Other syntax errors are only detected when you attempt to run the code. At that point, VBA halts code execution and highlights the line that generated the error.

Runtime errors

A runtime error occurs when a piece of code is attempting an operation that is impossible to execute, for example, trying to reference an object that is currently inaccessible, like a workbook that is currently closed. For errors like these, you can provide error handlers in your procedures to catch the error, display a meaningful message to the user, and gracefully exit the procedure.

Logic errors

Logic errors occur when there is nothing wrong with the syntax, but the application does not produce the intended result. As mentioned earlier, these errors are the difficult ones to find because the syntax is valid code, hence VBA will not halt the execution of the code. The code will run as normal but simply not produce your expected result. This type of error is caused by a logic error in one or more of your statements. Often, the only way to identify the source of the error is to put a breakpoint in your code and step through it line by line to observe the values of your variables and expressions at different points in the code.

Debugging Tools

VBA provides a wide array of debugging tools that can help you to find and correct errors in your code. You can use debugging tools like breakpoints, procedure stepping, watching variables, and the call stack to see the order of procedure execution.

The debugging menu items can be found under the **Debug** menu of the Visual Basic Editor. There is also a separate Debug toolbar that you can display by right-clicking the Visual Basic Editor menu bar and selecting the **Debug** checkbox from the pop-up menu.

The figure below shows the buttons on the Debug toolbar in the Visual Basic Editor.

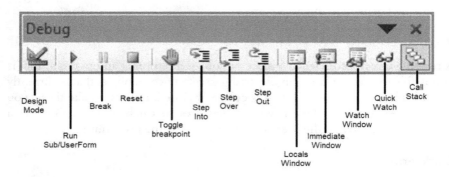

Tip: The Debug menu initially displays as a floating menu, but you can dock it to the Visual Basic Editor menu bar by dragging it over the space to the right of the default menu commands.

Break Mode

Break mode pauses code execution at the line where you have inserted a breakpoint. At this point, the program is still running but it is paused. While in break mode, you can examine the current values in the variables, properties, and expressions that are in scope. You can also choose to step through your code one line at a time, to examine the program flow and how any variables and properties are being changed. This is one of the most effective ways of quickly identifying logic errors in your code.

In break mode, the following actions occur:

- **Execution is paused**

  When VBA encounters a condition that causes it to enter break mode, it will stop code execution and switch control to the Visual Basic Editor.

- **Variables and properties are preserved**

  As the code is still effectively running but just paused, the variables and properties are preserved. Hence, you can check the current values of variables, properties, and expressions. You can change the values of variables and properties to observe the effect on other objects. You can also call other procedures.

You can enter break mode by doing the following:

- **Set a breakpoint**

  You use this to pause the execution of an application in a specific line in your code.

- **Use any of the Step commands on the Debug menu**

  When you use one of the **Step** commands, executing starts but then VBA enters break mode at the beginning of the procedure. This allows you to step through the code using one of the **Step** commands.

Setting a Breakpoint

You can set a breakpoint by either using the **Breakpoint** feature or using the **Stop** statement in your code. When code execution reaches that point, it will enter break mode.

To set a breakpoint in your code, do the following:

1. Position the insertion point anywhere in the line where you want execution to be paused in the procedure.

   Note: You can't select a line that's a comment or a variable declaration as you can't put a breakpoint on those lines.

2. On the Visual Basic Editor menu bar, click **Debug** and select **Toggle Breakpoint** from the menu (or press F9).

—or—

Click next to the statement on the Margin Indicator Bar (if visible).

—or—

On the Visual Basic Editor **Debug** toolbar, click the **Toggle Breakpoint** button.

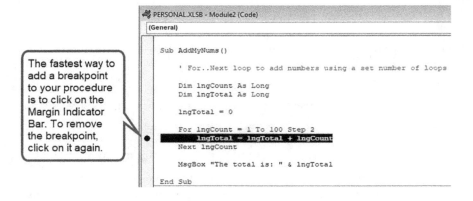

To clear a breakpoint, do the following:

Place the insertion point anywhere in the line in the procedure containing the breakpoint and repeat any of the commands described above for setting a breakpoint.

—or—

To clear all breakpoints in your project, on the **Debug** menu, click **Clear All Breakpoints** (or press **Ctrl+Shift+F9**).

Note: Breakpoints, like the ones created above, are not preserved when you save and close the project. If you want breakpoints that remain available when you close and reopen your project, use the **Stop** statement anywhere in the code where you want to enter break mode. Just remember to remove all **Stop** statements when you're done with debugging.

Stepping Through Code

After you've entered break mode using one of the methods described above, you can step through the code using the Debug toolbar in the Visual Basic Editor. This method enables you to execute one line of code at a time and observe the results. If you are new to programming, this is particularly useful as you can observe the program flow and better understand how programming constructs like conditional statements and loops work.

The following section describes the three **Step** buttons on the Debug toolbar and how each one works.

- **Step Into**

  This button executes the code, one line at a time. When you click the Step Into button, it will highlight the next line to be executed. When you click the button again, it will execute that line, and then highlight the next and so on. Note that, you can just click on this button to start the process of stepping through the code without needing to set a breakpoint.

- **Step Over**

  This is like Step Into, but when execution comes across a statement that contains a call to another procedure (i.e. a nested procedure), it executes the procedure as a unit and then steps to the next statement in the current procedure. So, code execution does not branch into the nested procedure, rather, it stays within the current procedure. Use this if you have a lot of nested procedures in your code and you don't want the debugger to step into them.

- **Step Out**

  The Step Out command executes the remaining lines in the current procedure. If the procedure was called from within another procedure, then execution goes back to the calling procedure.

To step through your code one line at a time, using **Step Into**, do the following:

1. Enter break mode, using one of the methods described previously.

2. On the **Debug** menu, click **Step Into**. Continue to click the **Step Into** button to run each line of code.

—or—

3. Press F8 to run the next line of code. Continue pressing F8 to run the code, one line at a time.

Using the Immediate Window

You can use the Immediate window to display information from your program while it's in break mode. For example, you can use it to display the output from debugging statements in your code, like Debug.Print. You can use the Immediate window to check the current value of variables, properties, or statements, by typing them directly into the Immediate window. You can also use the Immediate window to experiment by assigning new values to variables and properties to see how they affect other variables, properties or objects in your code.

When you first open the Visual Basic Editor, the Immediate window may not be visible as it is not one of the windows opened by default.

To display the Immediate window at any time, do the following:

- On the Visual Basic Editor menu bar, click on **View** and select **Immediate Window** from the menu.

  —or—

- Click the **Immediate Window** button on the **Debug** toolbar.

  —or—

- Press Ctrl+G.

The following image shows how to view the value of a variable, *lngTotal*, and the value of an expression, *lngTotal + lngCount*. The procedure in which they're located is in break mode. You type a question mark, followed by the statement you want to evaluate, and then press Enter. The result will be displayed in the line below it.

```
Immediate

?lngTotal
 9
? lngTotal + lngCount
 14
```

The question mark is short for the VBA **Print** statement. You can equally use:

```
Print lngTotal
```

However, a question mark in place of Print is faster and cleaner.

```
? lngTotal
```

The Immediate window's scope is limited to the current procedure or variables available to it, which include:

- Local variables declared in the procedure currently in break mode.

- Variables declared at the module level and available to all procedures in the current module.

- Variables declared at the project level, also known as *global variables* and available to all procedures in the project.

Variables or properties that are out of scope can't be accessed in the Immediate window.

Using the Debug.Print Statement

One way to monitor what is happening to variables in your code at runtime is to insert the **Print** method of the **Debug** object in your code to send an output to the Immediate window.

For instance, you may want to view the history of a variable or property as the program runs. You can use **Debug.Print** to track the value of the variable or property at each stage in your code by sending outputs to the Immediate window. When code execution pauses or completes, you can then review the printed values in the Immediate window.

In the following example, the **Debug.Print** statement prints the value of lngTotal in the Immediate window with each iteration of the loop.

```
Sub AddNumbers()
    Dim lngCount As Long
    Dim lngTotal As Long

    lngTotal = 0

    For lngCount = 1 To 10
        lngTotal = lngTotal + lngCount
        Debug.Print lngTotal
    Next lngCount

End Sub
```

Using the Locals Window

You can use the Locals window to monitor the values of variables while your application is running. The Locals window shows the variables declared in your procedure and the value they currently hold.

For example, if you are stepping through your code, you could use the Locals window to observe how the variables are changing. This could help you determine when an error was introduced due to a variable change, and what action caused it to happen.

The Locals window displays the information in three columns:

- **Expression**

  The expression column lists the name of the variables. You can't change the data in this column.

- **Value**

  This column lists the values of variables. You can edit the values here to test how your code responds to the new values.

- **Type**

  The type column contains the data type of the variables. You can't change the data in this column.

To display the Locals window, do the following:

- On the Visual Basic Editor menu bar, click **View** and select **Locals Window** from the menu.

  —or—

- Click the **Locals Window** button on the **Debug** toolbar.

Using the Watch Window

The Watch window is used to monitor expressions as your code runs. Unlike the Locals window that you can use to observe your variables as your code runs, you can use to watch window to observe whole expressions that you enter in the window. The expression can be a variable, a call to a function, or any other valid expression.

To display your Watch window, do the following:

- On the Visual Basic Editor menu bar, click on **View** and select **Watch Window** from the menu.

  —or—

- Click the **Watch Window** button on the Debug toolbar.

Adding a Watch Expression

There are three types of watch expressions in VBA.

- **Watch Expression**

  This displays the expression you're watching and its value in the Watch window when your program enters break mode.

- **Break When Value Is True**

  This option causes VBA to enter break mode when the expression you're watching becomes true during code execution. This helps you to determine the point at which an expression passes a test and what happens next.

- **Break When Value Changes**

  This type of Watch expression causes VBA to enter break mode if the value of the variable or property changes from its initial value. This helps when you want to observe exactly when a variable or property changes and what caused the change.

To add a Watch expression, do the following:

1. On the Visual Basic Editor menu bar, click **Debug** and select **Add Watch** from the menu.

2. In the **Expression** text box, enter the expression that you want to monitor.

3. Under **Context**, select the procedure or module name that you want to set as the scope for the watch expression using the Procedure and Module drop-down lists.

4. Under **Watch Type**, select the Watch type you want to create from the three options. This determines how VBA will respond to the watch expression.

5. Click **OK** when done.

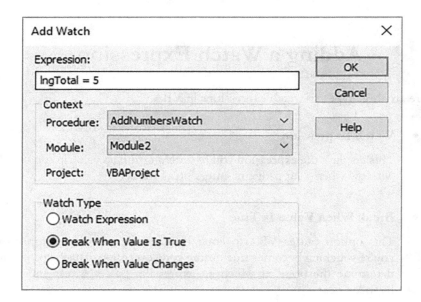

Tip: A watch expression can be particularly useful when you have a loop with a lot of iterations and you want to enter break mode near the end of the loop counter. Using **Step Into** to step through the code can be time-consuming for a very large loop. With the Watch window, you can set an expression that watches the loop counter and then breaks when it reaches a certain value.

The Call Stack

The Call Stack is a debugging tool that's useful for more complex projects with several nested Sub procedure or function calls. If you're calling procedures in your code that are themselves calling other procedures, the hierarchy of procedure calls could become complex.

Let's say you have one procedure call another procedure, and then within the second procedure you call a third procedure, and all this is happening before the first procedure has finished running. Just like a complex hierarchy of nested Excel formulas, it could become difficult to keep track of several levels of nested procedure calls, depending on how complex your application is. The Call Stack helps by showing the flow of execution through procedures.

To debug your code, you may want to keep track of the order that the procedures are being called. With the Call stack, you can verify that your code follows the correct sequence of procedures.

The following image shows three nested procedures in the Call Stack window.

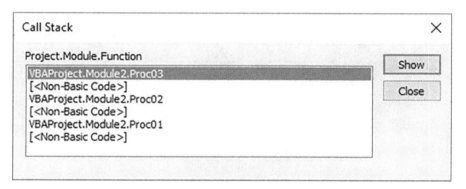

The last procedure executed, *Proc03*, is the first one to appear in the Call Stack, while the first procedure executed, *Proc01*, appears at the bottom of the list.

At any point during your debugging, you can examine the Call Stack if the program flow has gone through several procedures.

Note that you can only display the call stack window when your code is in break mode.

To display the Call Stack, do the following:

- While your code is in break mode, on the **View** menu of the Visual Basic Editor, click on **Call Stack** to display the Call Stack.

  —or—

- Click the **Call Stack** button on the Debug menu.

7. THE EXCEL OBJECT MODEL

As you use Excel, you probably see the workbooks, worksheets, and ranges as part of the application and not as individual objects. Internally, however, Excel treats these parts as individual, self-contained, objects in a hierarchical model called the Excel object model. You can take advantage of these objects to create VBA solutions without having to write too much code.

In this chapter, we will cover:

- An overview of the Excel object model.
- How to declare an object variable and assign an object to it.
- Object properties and methods.
- How to set properties.
- How to call methods.
- Using the **With...End With** statement with objects.

Objects and Collections

In programming or software, objects are packaged functionality with a defined set of behaviours (known as methods in VBA) and characteristics (known as properties in VBA). You can put various objects together to create solutions programmatically.

A collection is an object that groups several related objects together so that they can be programmatically controlled as a unit. A collection can have zero or more related objects. For example, there is a **Worksheets** collection which can hold several **Worksheet** objects. Each Worksheet object in the collection has its own properties and methods. However, the Worksheets collection also has its own properties and methods that you can use to control multiple Worksheet objects within it as a single unit.

The Object Hierarchy

The Excel object model is a structured model with different objects organised into a hierarchy based on the relationships between the objects. The object model defines which objects are exposed and how they relate to each other. The highest object in the hierarchy is **Application**, which represents the Excel application itself.

The image below shows a subset of the Excel object model. A rectangle represents a collection of objects and an oval represents a single object.

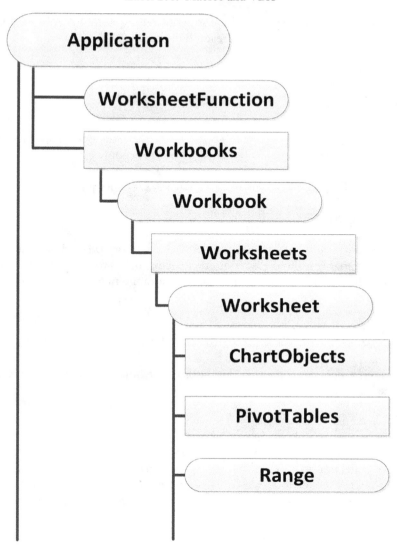

Note: For a complete listing of the Excel object model, visit Excel's VBA help with the link below:

https://docs.microsoft.com/en-us/office/vba/api/overview/excel/object-model

You can use the pre-packaged functionality in Excel objects to create custom solutions without having to write the code from scratch. For example, you may want to create a solution that uses the PivotTable object in Excel to display data to the user. You don't have to write the code to create a pivot table from scratch.

That would be way too daunting! Instead, you can declare a PivotTable object and access the functionality that's already built into it.

Declaring an Object

To create an instance of an object to access its methods and properties, you must first declare it as an object variable in your procedure.

For example, the following code declares **rngVAT** as a Range object variable:

```
Dim rngVAT As Range
```

If you intend to use an object in multiple places in your code, you can assign it to an object variable using the **Set** command. This makes for a cleaner and more efficient code. The following example assigns a range named Vat to a variable using **Set**:

```
Set rngVAT = Workbooks("AnnualFigures.xlsx") _
    Worksheets("Sheet1").Range("Vat")
```

We can then access properties and methods of the object using the variable, like in the example below:

```
rngVAT.Value = 0.2
```

You can also declare an object variable and use it in a **For...Each** loop to iterate through a collection to access instances of the object. In the example below, we loop through a collection (which is a range of selected cells) and use a Debug.Print statement to display the value of each cell in the Immediate window.

```
Dim rngCell As Range

For Each rngCell In Selection.Cells
     Debug.Print rngCell.Value
Next rngCell
```

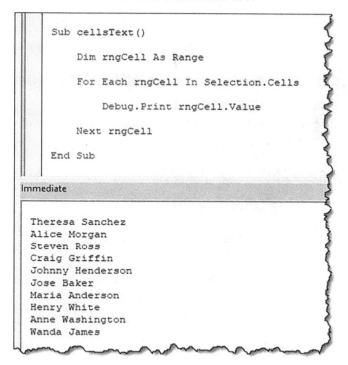

```
Sub cellsText()

    Dim rngCell As Range

    For Each rngCell In Selection.Cells

        Debug.Print rngCell.Value

    Next rngCell

End Sub
```

Immediate

```
Theresa Sanchez
Alice Morgan
Steven Ross
Craig Griffin
Johnny Henderson
Jose Baker
Maria Anderson
Henry White
Anne Washington
Wanda James
```

Properties and Methods

To access the functionality provided by objects, you work with properties and methods.

Properties

Properties are a set of characteristics of an object. For example, the Worksheet object has properties like **Name** and **Visible**.

Methods

Methods are behaviours that an object can exhibit. These are actions that you can carry out with an object. For example, the Worksheet object has methods like **ShowAllData**, **Protect** and **Calculate**.

Tip: To get a detailed list of the methods and properties of an Excel object. Use the format "*object name* properties" or "*object name* methods" to search for it in your search engine, where *object name* is the name of the object for which you want help. One of the top search results will be the official VBA help page for that object.

Setting Properties and Calling Methods

To change the characteristics or attributes of an object, you change its properties by assigning different values to them. Methods, on the other hand, cause an object to carry out an action or a task. Hence, you use methods to perform actions and use properties to set or retrieve attributes of an object.

Setting Properties

To set a property of an object in code, use the following syntax:

Object.Property = Value

The following example assigns **True** to the **Bold** property of the **Font** object of the selected range. This bolds the text in that range.

```
Selection.Font.Bold = True
```

To turn off bold you can set the property to **False**, like this.

```
Selection.Font.Bold = True
```

Calling Methods

The way you invoke methods in your code will depend on whether the method returns a value and if that value will be used in your procedure. You can think of methods as verbs. For example, you can *open* a *door*. So, if we were to translate that to VBA code, it would be:

```
Door.Open
```

Some methods return a value and others don't. Also, some methods have parameters and others don't.

Note: A **parameter** is a variable that is part of a method's definition or syntax. When you call the method in your code, the values you pass into the parameters are called **arguments**. These terms are sometimes used interchangeably.

If you don't want to use the value returned by a method, or if the method doesn't return a value, then use the syntax below to call it. Note that the arguments are optional as not all methods have parameters.

Object.Method [arg1, arg2, ...]

An example of a method that does not have a parameter or a return value is the **Select** method of the **Range** object:

```
Range("A1:A10").Select
```

The following statement runs the **AutoFit** method of the **Columns** collection to auto-fit the text in the selected columns.

```
Selection.Columns.AutoFit
```

If a method returns a value, then you call it by assigning the return value to a variable.

If the method has parameters, then you place parentheses around the arguments when you call it. You generally want to use parentheses any time the method appears to the right of the equal sign.

Use the following syntax to call a method when you want to assign the return value to a variable:

Variable = Object.Method([arg1, arg2, ...])

You can also explicitly define a parameter by assigning an argument directly to its name when you call the method. The following example copies data from cells A1:A4 on Sheet1 to cells B1:B4 on Sheet1. You can see that the *Destination* parameter was explicitly defined.

```
Sub CopyAndPaste()
    Worksheets("Sheet1").Range("A1:A4").Copy
    ActiveSheet.Paste
Destination:=Worksheets("Sheet1").Range("B1:B4")
End Sub
```

Using the With...End With Statement

The **With...End With** statement is something you will encounter often when you're editing macros generated by the macro recorder. This statement is used primarily to access properties and methods of objects.

When you access properties and call methods, you will often write several statements that perform actions on the same object. You can use the **With...End With** statement to make the code run more efficiently as you're referencing the object name just once.

The following piece of code sets various formatting options for the selected range in Excel using the **With...End With** statement.

```
Sub UsingWith()
' Formats the selected range in the active worksheet.
    With Selection.Font
         .Name = "Calibri"
         .Size = 20
         .Bold = True
         .Italic = True
         .Underline = True
    End With
End Sub
```

8. EDITING RECORDED MACROS

Now that we've covered the necessary VBA skills that you need to edit your macros, we can dive right into editing recorded macros. If a macro you've recorded is not behaving the way you want it to, you don't necessarily need to record it again. It is often better to edit the source code in the Visual Basic Editor to make the necessary corrections. Sometimes just viewing the source code may help you to quickly identify and fix simple errors or to see where minor adjustments need to be made. Even if you choose to re-record the macro, viewing the source code of the previous recording may give you an idea of what went wrong and how to fix that when recording it again.

In this chapter, we will cover:
- Opening your macro's source code from Excel and from Visual Basic.
- Editing your macro in the Visual Basic Editor.
- How to insert an InputBox function in your macro to make it interactive.
- How to Find and Replace text in your macro.
- How to handle error messages that can pop up when you try to run your macro.
- Saving your changes to ensure you don't lose your work.

There are two ways you can view your macro's VBA code:

- **Method 1**: Open your macro from within Excel. Unhide the Personal Macro Workbook, then select and open your macro with the Macro dialog box.

- **Method 2**: Open your macro from Visual Basic. Open the Visual Basic Editor, then in the Project window, locate and open your macro in the code window.

Viewing Your Macro's Source Code from Excel

Note: If the macro you want to edit is stored in your Personal Macro Workbook you first need to unhide this workbook before you can edit any macros stored in it.

Follow the steps below to open your macro's source code from Excel:

1. Click the **View** tab, then click the **Unhide** command button.

   Excel displays the **Unhide** dialog box showing the PERSONAL.XLSB workbook in the Unhide Workbook list.

2. Select **PERSONAL.XLSB** in the list box and click on **OK** to unhide the workbook.

   With the Personal Macro Workbook unhidden, you can now edit its macros from within your working file. Minimise PERSONAL.XLSB and return to your initial workbook.

3. On the **View** tab, click the drop-down arrow on the **Macros** command button, then select **View Macros** from the drop-down list.

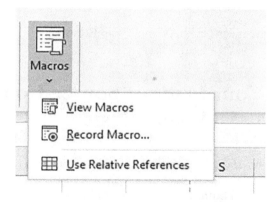

This opens the **Macro** dialog box showing the names of the macros that you've created in the active workbook and all other open workbooks.

4. In the **Macros in** drop-down list, ensure **All Open Workbooks** is selected.

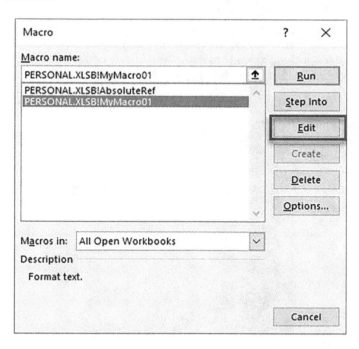

5. In the **Macro Name** list box, select the macro name that you want to edit and then click the **Edit** button. If your macro is stored in the Personal Macro Workbook, it will be prefixed with PERSONAL.XLSB.

Excel will display the macro in the Visual Basic Editor.

Viewing Your Macro's Source Code from Visual Basic

A faster way to open and edit your macro, without needing to first unhide the Personal Macro Workbook (if your macro is stored there), is to click on the **Visual Basic** command button on the **Developer** tab to open the Visual Basic Editor.

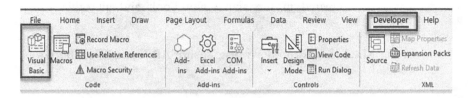

Once the Visual Basic Editor is open, in the Project window, expand the **Modules** folder and locate your macro name in one of the modules. To locate your macro, double-click a module to display its contents in the code window on the right.

The macro name should start with a statement like this:

Sub *MacroName*()

(where *MacroName* is the name you gave the macro when recording it)

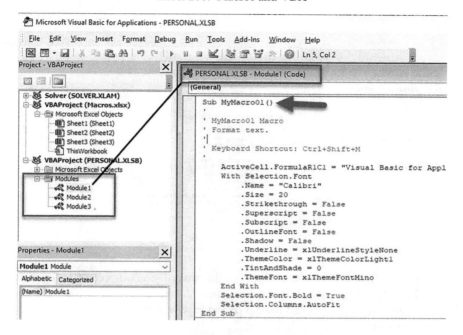

If you have more than one module, double click them to display their content until you find the one that contains the macro you want to edit. Ideally, you want to start with the latest module created because a recently created macro is likely to be located in one of the latest modules.

If your macro is saved in your current Excel file, that is, an XLSM file, then the macro will be saved in a module under your worksheet name in the Project window.

Editing Your Macro

Once you have the macro open in the code window, you can now make changes to the macro. The code for the macro we created in chapter one is stored in a **Sub** procedure named *MyMacro1* (or the name you gave your macro when you created it). The ending statement of the macro is denoted with the **End Sub** statement. To make changes to the macro, ensure you keep your edits within this area.

You'll notice that the first few lines of the macro contain commented text. These include the name of the macro, any description you entered in the Description box in the Record Macro dialog box, and the keyboard shortcut (if any was assigned).

In the following example, we will open and edit the macro we created in Chapter 1. The macro name is *MyMacro01*.

We will amend the macro by:

- Changing the text to: "Visual Basic for Applications"
- Increasing the font to 20 points

Current macro code:

```
Sub MyMacro01()
'
' MyMacro01 Macro
' Format text.
'
' Keyboard Shortcut: Ctrl+Shift+M
'
    ActiveCell.FormulaR1C1 = "Microsoft Excel Macros"
    With Selection.Font
        .Name = "Calibri"
        .Size = 14
        .Strikethrough = False
        .Superscript = False
        .Subscript = False
        .OutlineFont = False
```

```
      .Shadow = False
      .Underline = xlUnderlineStyleNone
      .ThemeColor = xlThemeColorLight1
      .TintAndShade = 0
      .ThemeFont = xlThemeFontMinor
   End With
   Selection.Font.Bold = True
   Selection.Columns.AutoFit
End Sub
```

Follow the steps below to edit the macro above:

1. Change the text "Microsoft Excel Macros" to "Visual Basic for Applications"

2. Change size (.Size) from 14 to 20.

The lines with the changes should look like this:

```
ActiveCell.FormulaR1C1 = "Visual Basic for Applications"

.Size = 20
```

All the other lines remain the same.

3. After making your changes, click the **Save** button on the Visual Basic Editor toolbar (the blue disk icon).

4. Click the **View Microsoft Excel** button (at the beginning of the toolbar) to return to your workbook.

5. In a blank worksheet, select cell A1, then run the modified macro (either by pressing its shortcut keys, or opening the **Macro** dialog box and running it from there).

If the macro doesn't work as intended, you need to return to the Visual Basic Editor to locate and correct any errors. Clicking the **Visual Basic** command button on the **Developer** tab of the Ribbon will return you to the Visual Basic Editor where you can edit the code again.

If all goes well, the macro would enter in cell A1 the text "Visual Basic for Applications", with font size 20, bolded, and AutoFit applied to the column.

6. To close the Visual Basic Editor, simply click on the **Close** button on the top right of the window (x icon). You can also close the window by clicking on **File > Close and Return to Microsoft Excel**.

Saving Your Changes

It can be easy to lose new macros or changes to existing macros when they're stored in the hidden PERSONAL.XLSB file. If you mistakenly close Excel without saving the Personal Macro Workbook, you would lose all the changes you made to it. And it can be easy to close Excel without saving PERSONAL.XLSB because it is a hidden file. AutoSave does not work in this regard.

If you saved your changes using the **Save** button on the Visual Basic Editor toolbar, then that will save the modifications you've made to your macro. However, if you closed the Visual Basic Editor without saving your work, you can still save your changes in Excel.

If you stored your macro as part of the current workbook, click the **Save** button on the Quick Access Toolbar to save the changes to the modified macro.

If the modified macro was saved in the Personal Macro Workbook, when you try to exit Excel, a dialog box will ask you if you want to save the changes you made to the Personal Macro Workbook. It can be easy to dismiss this dialog box without reading the message hence lose any changes to the PERSONAL.XLSB file.

When prompted to save the file, ensure you click the **Save** button to save your macro modifications as you close down Excel.

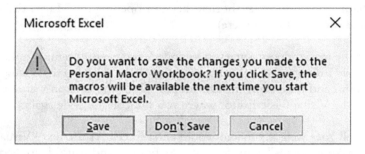

If you close Excel without saving it here the changes will be discarded.

Using the InputBox Function to make your Macro Interactive

One of the problems with the macro we recorded in chapter 1 is that the text we're inserting in our worksheet is hardcoded in the macro. This means there is no way of changing that text unless the macro is edited, making the macro limited for situations where we could have different headings. For that, we would need a macro that allows us to enter the information when the macro runs. That is, essentially, to make the macro interactive. This is where the InputBox function comes in.

The InputBox function displays a dialog box with a textbox that allows you to enter text when the macro runs.

The InputBox has the following syntax:

InputBox(prompt, [title], [default], [xpos], [ypos], [helpfile, context])

Below are descriptions of the arguments and what they mean:

Argument	Description
prompt	Required. This is the message that is displayed in the dialog box. This message can be a string, a number, or a date. It needs to be a maximum of 1024 characters. If the prompt message is too long, you can break it into multiple lines with the VBA keyword vbNewLine which inserts a carriage return in a line.
title	Optional. This is the title for the input box. If omitted, "Microsoft Excel" is placed in the title bar.
default	Optional. This is a default value that will appear in the text box when the dialog box is initially displayed. If you omit this argument, the text box is left blank.
xpos	Optional. This argument specifies the horizontal distance of the left edge of the dialog box from the left edge of the screen. If *xpos* is omitted, the dialog box will be in the centre horizontally.

ypos	Optional. This argument specifies the vertical distance of the upper edge of the dialog box from the top of the screen. If *ypos* is omitted, the dialog box's default position is approximately one-third of the way down the screen vertically.
helpfile	Optional. This argument identifies the Help file to use to provide Help for the dialog box that is context-sensitive. If *helpfile* is provided, you must also provide *context*.
context	Optional. This is a number that the Help author assigned as the Help context number for the Help topic. If you provide *context*, you must also provide *helpfile*.

In its simplest form, you can use the InputBox with only the required argument, which is the *prompt*.

InputBox("Enter the worksheet title.")

Example:

To insert the InputBox function in the macro we created in chapter 1, do the following:

1.   Open the *MyMacro01* macro that we created in Chapter 1 and edited in this chapter (or any macro in which you can test the InputBox).

     On the **Developer** tab, click the **Visual Basic** command button and locate the Sub procedure named *MyMacro01* in one of the modules in the Modules folder.

2.   Edit the Sub procedure named *MyMacro01* and enter the following lines of code at the top of the subroutine (after the commented code).

```
txtPrompt = "Enter the title of the worksheet in the text
box below and click OK."
txtTitle = "Worksheet Title"
txtDefault = "Microsoft Excel Macros"
txtWorksheetTitle    =    InputBox(txtPrompt,    txtTitle,
txtDefault)
```

Here, we're are assigning values to variables and then using those variables as the arguments for the InputBox function.

Note: We can enter the values directly into the InputBox function as arguments, but the statement would be long and cumbersome, hence, it is best to assign them to variables, making the code neater and easier to read.

3. Next, replace the following line of code:

```
ActiveCell.FormulaR1C1 = "Visual Basic for
Applications"
```

with this line:

```
ActiveCell.FormulaR1C1 = txtWorksheetTitle
```

In the line, we're assigning the variable that stores the returned value from the InputBox to the active cell in the worksheet.

The image below shows how your finished code should look:

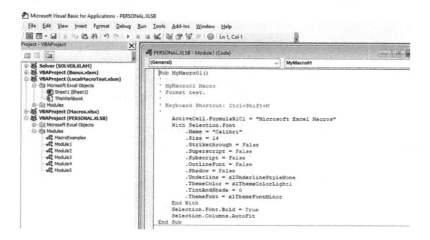

4. On the Visual Basic Editor, click on the **Save** command button to save your changes.

5. Return to Excel. Click the **View Microsoft Excel** button (Excel icon on the toolbar) to switch to your Excel worksheet.

6. Run the macro. Select cell A1 in your worksheet, and then click the **Macro** command button on the **Developer** tab. In the **Macros** dialog box, select and run the MyMacro01 macro (which should be named PERSONAL.XLSB!MyMacro01 if you saved it in the Personal Macro Workbook).

7. The input dialog box will be displayed with the default text we specified.

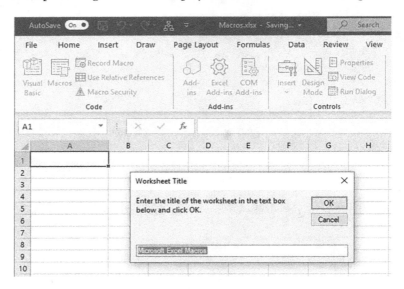

8. Enter "Visual Basic for Applications" in the text box (it will automatically replace Microsoft Excel Macros) and click **OK**.

Excel will enter the text in cell A1 and then carry out the other formatting tasks recorded in the macro.

Find and Replace Code in Your Macro

Usually, the best way to change text with several instances in your macro is to use the find and replace feature in the Visual Basic Editor. The find and replace feature enables you to replace all instances of a particular piece of text in a consistent way as you don't have to type the same text multiple times.

Finding Text

To open the Find dialog box, click **Edit** on the Visual Basic Editor toolbar, and then select **Find** from the menu.

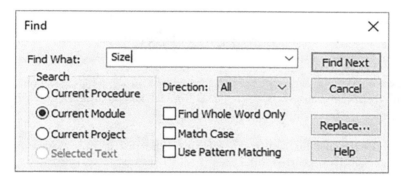

The Find dialog box allows you to find text or statements in your macro code. This is similar to the Find dialog box in your Excel workbook.

In this dialog box, there are different search options that you can select for the search:

- **Current Procedure**: Searches only the current procedure, which is essentially the current macro code your cursor is in.

- **Correct Module**: Searches all the macros in the current module you are in. This is the default option.

- **Current Project**: Searches all the modules in the current project. Usually, the project would be an excel workbook so this option will search all the modules in a particular workbook.

- **Selected Text**: This option is only enabled if you selected a block of code in the module. With a block of text selected, if you choose this option, the find action will be restricted to that block of text.

After entering the piece of text or statement as your search string in the **Find What** text box, select the search option you want to use, and click the **Find Next** button.

Excel will attempt to find the first occurrence of the search term in the code and then select it in the current procedure, module, VBA project, or selected text (depending on which option you selected).

To find the next occurrence of your search criteria, click the Find Next button again, and so on until all occurrences of the search term are found.

Replacing Text

If you want to find and replace text that appears in multiple places in your code, use the **Replace** dialog box. Using the Replace dialog box ensures that all occurrences are found and replaced.

To open the Replace dialog box, click **Edit** on the Visual Basic Editor toolbar, and then select **Replace** from the menu.

Note: You can also open the Replace dialog box by clicking the **Replace** button on the Find dialog box (if you already have it open).

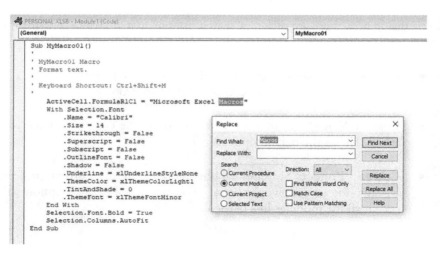

The Replace dialog box is similar to the find dialog box, but it gives you two text boxes - **Find What** and **Replace With**. The Find What box contains the text you want to find and the Replace With text box holds the replacement text.

To find and replace text, do the following:

1. Enter the text you want to find in the **Find What** text box and the replacement text in the **Replace With** text box.

2. Click the **Find Next** button to find the first instance of the text.

3. If you want to replace that instance, click the Replace button. If you don't want to replace it then click **Find Next** to skip that instance and go to the next one.

    When you click **Replace**, Excel will automatically find the next instance in the current procedure, module, VBA project, or selected text (depending on which option you selected).

4. Repeat steps 2 and 3 until you find and replace all instances of the text you want to replace.

Tip: To be on the safe side, avoid using the **Replace All** button because it might end up replacing some text you don't want to replace. It is important to be able to see every instance of the text you're replacing, otherwise, you could end up introducing errors in your code by replacing the wrong text. The search term could easily be used in a different context in the code and you don't want those ones changed. Using the combination of **Find Next** and **Replace** can be very fast even for a large amount of code.

Dealing with Error Messages from Your Macro

You may encounter an error when you run your newly created macro. This can happen whether you're new to VBA or even a veteran VBA programmer. If your macro encounters an error, VBA will display an error message… usually a cryptic message!

On some occasions, however, you would get a pointer to the problem from the error message. So, ensure you always read the error message before dismissing it. I know from experience that as the message can often be unhelpful, it's easy to get into the habit of dismissing it without even reading it. This could mean missing out on vital information that would enable you to resolve the problem faster.

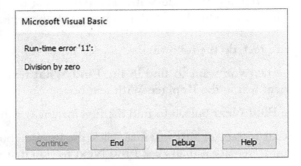

After reading the message, click the **Debug** button. This will dismiss the dialog box and open the Visual Basic Editor. Excel will highlight the line of code where the program failed. Sometimes the highlighted line would be what caused the error. On other occasions, the error was introduced before the point of failure and you would need to carry out an investigation to find it. When you identify the problem, edit the code, and fix it.

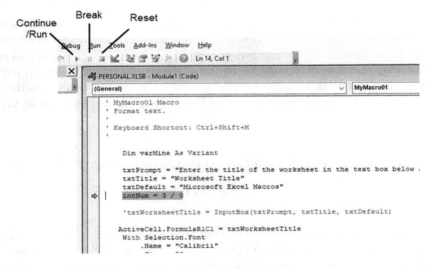

While in debug mode, the macro is still running. To stop the macro, click on the **Reset** button (this is the blue square icon on the toolbar). When you're done with editing the macro, save your work again by clicking **File** > **Save** on the menu bar (or the Save button on the toolbar – the blue disk icon).

Tip: You can click on the **Run** button on the toolbar (the blue right-pointing triangle) to run your macro from within the Visual Basic Editor. The process will switch to your Excel worksheet if your macro is referencing cells there.

9. CREATING USER-DEFINED FUNCTIONS

One of the best ways to make use of VBA is in creating user-defined functions that you can use in your worksheets just as you would use a built-in Excel function. User-defined functions are also referred to as 'custom functions' and these terms will be used interchangeably in this book.

In this chapter, we will cover:
- How to create a user-defined function.
- Adding a description to a user-defined function in the Object Browser.
- How to use a user-defined function as a formula in your workbook.
- How to save your user-defined function as an Excel Add-in.

Some Benefits of User-Defined Functions include:

- You don't need to run them the way you run macros. You can type them directly into a worksheet cell or insert them with the Insert Function button on the formula bar.

- You can carry out more complex evaluations, with more decisions, due to the increased flexibility a programming language offers you over a formula.

- It's easier to maintain complex calculations with multiple logical decisions in code compared to formulas. Excel formulas can become quite cumbersome and difficult to maintain if you incorporate too many logical decisions.

Creating a User Defined Function

Before we delve into creating a custom function, here are a few notes on functions that you need to be aware of:

- You can have between 0 and 255 arguments in a function.

- User-defined functions cannot be created with the macro recorder. They must be coded manually in VBA.

- A function needs to return a value. If you want to create a procedure that executes a piece of code but doesn't return a value, use a **Sub** procedure.

- There are two ways in which you can use a function once it has been created. You can either use it to calculate and return a value within another procedure or use it directly in your worksheet.

- The name of your custom function cannot duplicate any built-in function names in Excel like SUM, COUNT, or AVERAGE.

- You must list any arguments in parentheses, and in the order in which they are processed.

Custom Function Example

In this example, let's say we want to pay salespeople a bonus periodically based on a graduated scale. The bonus paid is based on the number of rentals they've sold for the period and the revenue generated. We want to create a function that carries out this calculation automatically when we pass in the input values.

Bonus levels

The bonus paid is on a graduated scale based on the number of rentals sold.

Number of rentals sold	Bonus (%)
1	1.5%
2 or more	2%
5 or more	3%
10 or more	4%

The data model below summarises the number of rentals sold, and the revenue generated by each estate agent.

	A	B	C	D	E	F
1	**Estate Agent Bonus**					
2						
3	**Estate Agent**	**# of Rentals**	**Revenue**	**Bonus**		
4	Theresa Sanchez	2	$6,176			
5	Alice Morgan	3	$7,875			
6	Steven Ross	4	$29,448			The
7	Craig Griffin	5	$22,178			function
8	Johnny Henderson	6	$50,882			will be
9	Jose Baker	2	$15,920			used
10	Maria Anderson	6	$113,687			here
11	Henry White	7	$115,538			
12	Anne Washington	1	$8,677			
13	Wanda James	12	$228,691			
14						

We now need to calculate the bonus to be paid to each estate agent in cells D4:D13 using our graduated bonus scale. This is where we will apply our custom formula.

After defining the problem, we have a better idea of the kind of function required for the solution. The function will take in two arguments (the number of rentals sold, and the revenue generated), and then return the calculated bonus:

Bonus(Rentals, Revenue)

Follow the steps below to create the function:

1. **Create a new module where your custom function will be defined.**

   Ideally, you want to save the custom function in the Personal Macro Workbook (which is hidden by default) and not in the workbook with your data.

   Open the Visual Basic Editor by clicking on the Visual Basic command button on the Developer tab. In Project Explorer, expand the tree of the VBAProject(PERSONAL.XLSB) object. Right-click **Modules** and choose **Insert > Module** from the shortcut menu.

   Once the new module has been created, double click the module name to open its code window.

2. **Enter the name of the function and specify the arguments.**

For this example, we'll be using *Bonus* for the function name with *intRentals* and *varRevenue* used as the name of the arguments.

In the code window, type the following statement and press enter:

```
Function Bonus(intRentals, varRevenue)
```

Visual Basic will automatically enter the end statement of the function:

```
End Function
```

3. **Enter the code that will calculate and return the bonus for each salesperson.**

For this example, I have used the **Select Case** conditional statement to test for and select the correct option, but an **If... Then... Else** statement can equally be used to achieve the same result. When you have several conditions to test, a Select Case statement provides a more elegant and efficient solution.

Between the opening and closing statements of the function, enter the code below.

```
Select Case intRentals
    Case Is >= 10
        Bonus = varRevenue * 0.04
    Case Is >= 5
        Bonus = varRevenue * 0.035
    Case Is >= 2
        Bonus = varRevenue * 0.02
    Case Is = 1
        Bonus = varRevenue * 0.015
End Select
```

The Select Case statement tests intRentals (which is the number of rentals sold that will be passed in as an argument) against the different cases.

The program starts from the top of the Select Case, and the block of code for the first **Case** test that evaluates to TRUE is executed. The result is assigned to Bonus as the return value of the function.

Once a return value is assigned to the name of the function, the program exits the function and returns the value. Your finished code should now look like the code in the image below.

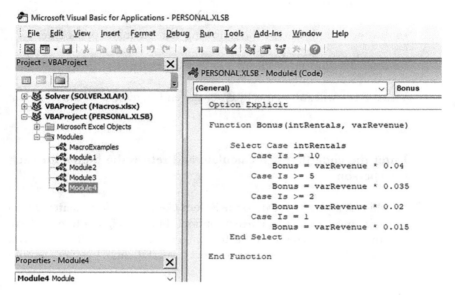

```
Function Bonus(intRentals, varRevenue)
    Select Case intRentals
        Case Is >= 10
            Bonus = varRevenue * 0.04
        Case Is >= 5
            Bonus = varRevenue * 0.035
        Case Is >= 2
            Bonus = varRevenue * 0.02
        Case Is = 1
            Bonus = varRevenue * 0.015
    End Select
End Function
```

4. **Save your custom function.**

Once you are done, you can save your custom function by clicking **File > Save** on the menu bar. Alternatively, you can click on the blue disk icon on the toolbar to save your work.

5. Click the **View Microsoft Excel** button on the toolbar to return to the worksheet where you want to use the custom function.

Note: This calculation could be done with an Excel formula using multiple nested functions, but a single user-defined function provides a neater and more efficient solution.

Tip: If you want to be able to use your custom function in any spreadsheet on your computer, ensure you create the function in your Personal Macro Workbook which is VBAProject(PERSONAL.XLSB) in Project Explorer. On the other hand, if you want the custom function to be only available to an individual workbook, then create a new module under the project for that workbook in Project Explorer. Note that if you add a module to a standard Excel workbook, you'll need to save the file as a Macro-Enabled Workbook (.xlsm).

Adding a Description to a User-Defined Function

After creating the function, the next task is to add descriptions that show up in the Insert Function and Function Arguments dialog boxes. This helps to explain what the function does when a user uses the Insert Function command to insert it in their worksheet.

To add this description, we need to use the Object Browser, which is a dialog box in the Visual Basic Editor that allows you to view information about the particular objects available to the currently active project.

Follow the steps below to add a description for your user-defined function:

1. If you're in Excel, open the Visual Basic Editor by clicking the Visual Basic command button on the Developer tab.

2. Navigate to the project where you stored your user-defined function and ensure this is the selected project in Project Explorer. In the case of the function we created in this chapter, this would be VBAProject (PERSONAL.XLSB).

3. On the Visual Basic Editor menu bar, click **View** > **Object Browser** (or press F2) to open the Object Browser window.

4. At the top left of the dialog box, you'll see a drop-down list box that currently has the value <All Libraries>. Click this drop-down list box and select **VBAProject** from the drop-down list.

5. Under **Classes**, on the left pane of the dialog box, you'll see a list of items including all the modules in the currently selected project. Click the module where you stored your user-defined function, and on the right pane, you'll see your function.

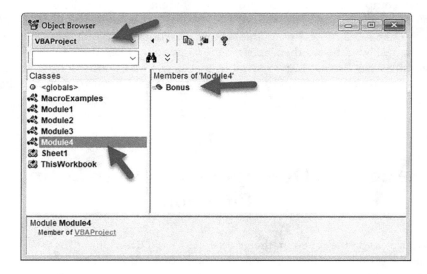

6. Right-click the name of your user-defined function and select **Properties** from the shortcut menu. This will open the **Member Options** dialog box.

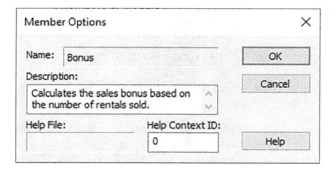

7. In the **Description** text box of the Member Options dialog box, enter the text that you want to appear in the Insert Function and Function Arguments dialog boxes in Excel when users select your user-defined function.

8. Click **OK** when done to save your changes, then, click the Close button on the Object Browser.

9. Save your changes by clicking **File** > **Save** on the Visual Basic Editor menu bar.

10. On the Visual Basic Editor toolbar, click the **View Microsoft Excel** command button to return to Excel. In Excel, click the **Save** button on the quick access toolbar.

You are now ready to use your function in your Excel workbook.

Note:
The custom function description does not always show up in the Insert Function and Function Arguments dialog boxes immediately after creation. You may need to save your Excel workbook, then close and restart Excel to have the description show up.

If the description still does not show up after restarting Excel, go through steps 1-6 above again to check that the text you entered for the description was indeed saved. If the description wasn't saved, then continue with steps 7-10 above to re-enter the description and save it again.

Using a User-Defined Function in Your Worksheet

To use your custom function, you can insert it into your worksheets with the **Insert Function** button on the **Formula** bar, just as you would do with built-in Excel functions.

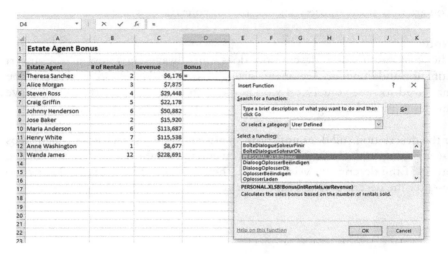

To use a user-defined function do the following:

1. On your worksheet, select the cell where you want to enter the formula.

2. On the **Formulas** tab, in the **Function Library** group, click the **Insert Function** command button to open the Insert Function dialog box.

3. In the Insert Function dialog box, select **User Defined** in the category drop-down list.

4. In the **Select a function** list box, locate your function and then select it.

   In the area under the list box, you'll see a description of the function and the arguments it takes. For the function we created in this chapter, the name would be **PERSONAL.XLSB!Bonus**. Note that the prefix indicates that the function is in the Personal Macro Workbook.

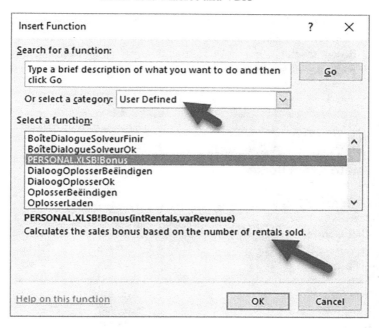

5. Click **OK** to open the **Function Arguments** dialog box. The Function Arguments dialog box enables you to enter the arguments by selecting the cells directly on your worksheet.

6. For our custom function, click in **IntRentals** and select cell B4 on the worksheet. Then click in **VarRevenue** and select C4 on the worksheet.

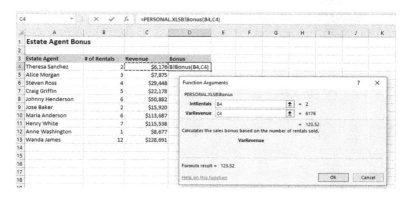

Note that the Functions Arguments dialog box gives you a preview of the result of the evaluation, based on the values entered as arguments.

7. Click OK to accept the values and enter the function.

8. If you're happy with the result returned in the first cell (in this case that would be cell D4), click on the fill handle of the cell and drag the values down to the other cells in the column to populate them with the formula. This would be cells D5:D13 in our example.

D13			✕ ✓ fx	=PERSONAL.XLSB!Bonus(B13,C13)	

	A	B	C	D	E
1	**Estate Agent Bonus**				
2					
3	**Estate Agent**	**# of Rentals**	**Revenue**	**Bonus**	
4	Theresa Sanchez	2	$6,176	$123.52	
5	Alice Morgan	3	$7,875	$157.50	
6	Steven Ross	4	$29,448	$588.96	
7	Craig Griffin	5	$22,178	$776.23	
8	Johnny Henderson	6	$50,882	$1,780.87	
9	Jose Baker	2	$15,920	$318.40	
10	Maria Anderson	6	$113,687	$3,979.05	
11	Henry White	7	$115,538	$4,043.83	
12	Anne Washington	1	$8,677	$130.16	
13	Wanda James	12	$228,691	$9,147.64	
14					
15					

With that, you have successfully created and used your bespoke function to carry out a specific calculation for which there was no built-in Excel function.

Saving a User-Defined Function as an Add-In

It is great that we're able to create a custom function that performs a specific calculation for our data. However, as you may have noticed in the previous section, there is a slight limitation. We stored the function in the Personal Macro Workbook, which means Excel adds the PERSONAL.XLSB prefix to the function name. For example, PERSONAL.XLSB!Bonus(B4, C4).

It would be better if we could just refer to the function name – Bonus, without the lengthy and confusing prefix just like all the built-in functions in Excel. Thankfully, there is a way to do this in Excel. We can remove the prefix by saving the workbook containing the custom function as an Excel add-in file. After doing that, we can then use the function by just typing the function name in the formula bar or selecting it from the Insert Function dialog box.

To save the workbook that contains your custom function as an Excel add-in file, follow the steps below:

1. **First, unhide the Personal Macro Workbook.**

   On the View tab of the ribbon, click the **Unhide** button, then select PERSONAL from the list and click **OK**.

2. **Open the Visual Basic Editor.**

   On the **Developer** tab of Excel's Ribbon, click the **Visual Basic** command button to open the Visual Basic Editor.

   In the Visual Basic Editor, select the project that contains your user-defined function in the Project window. For our example, the project name is VBAProject(PERSONAL.XLSB).

3. **Open VBAProject – Project Properties.**

   On the Visual Basic Editor menu bar, click **Tools > VBAProject Properties**.

   This opens the **VBAProject – Project Properties** dialog box. This dialog box has two tabs - General and Protection.

4. **Lock the project file to prevent unauthorised changes to the add-in.**

On the **VBAProject – Project Properties** dialog box, click the **Protection** tab and select the checkbox next to **Lock project for viewing**.

Locking the project for viewing ensures only authorised users can view and make changes to the project.

5. **Enter a password to protect the locked status.**

Enter a password to the **Password** text box and re-enter the password in the **Confirm password** text box, then click **OK** to confirm your changes.

This prevents other users from removing the protection status.

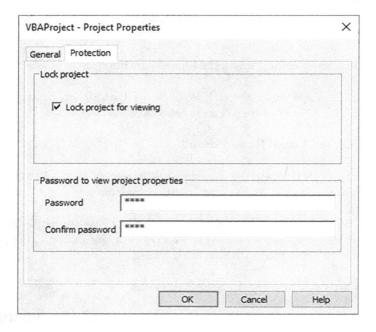

Important! You will be prompted for a password to view this project after you close and reopen the PERSONAL.XLSB file. Hence it is important that you enter a password you can remember. It is recommended that you write it down somewhere and keep it in a safe place for easy retrieval if needed. If you forget the password, there are no available tools provided by Microsoft that will enable you to access the project.

To remove the password at any point in the future:
1. In Project Explorer, logon to the project using the password.
2. Navigate to the **VBAProject – Project Properties** dialog box (as described above).
3. On the **Protection** tab, delete the passwords entered in the **Password** and **Confirm** password text boxes.
4. Uncheck **Lock project for viewing**.
5. Click **OK**.

6. **Save your changes**.

On the Visual Basic Editor toolbar, click the **Save** button. We now need to return to Excel to configure the add-in.

7. Click the **View Microsoft Excel** button on the Visual Basic Editor toolbar to return to your Excel worksheet.

8. **Give your add-in a name**.

Before saving the file as an add-in, we need to give it a title that is displayed as the add-in name in the list of add-ins in Excel Options.

In the PERSONAL.XLSB workbook (or the workbook in which you stored your custom function), click **File** to go to the Backstage view, and then click **Info**.

Excel will display the **Info** screen. On the right side of the Info screen, under **Properties**, click the textbox next to **Title** and enter the name that you want to give the add-in, and then press **Enter**. For our custom function created in this chapter, the name would be *Bonus Add-in*.

Properties ˅

Size	18.6KB
Title	Bonus Add-in
Tags	Add a tag
Comments	Add comments
Template	
Status	Add text
Categories	Add a category
Subject	Specify the subject
Hyperlink Base	Add text
Company	Specify the company

9. **Save the file as an add-in**.

After adding a Title property to the document, you will have a **Save As** option on the menu (on the left of the Backstage view). Click on **Save As**.

Excel will display the Save As screen with the XLSTART folder location currently selected as the location where it would be saved. Change the file type to an Excel add-in by clicking the drop-down button for the file type, and then selecting **Excel Add-in (*.xlam)** from the drop-down list.

Note that, after choosing to save the file as an Excel Add-in, the file location will be changed to … AppData > Roaming > Microsoft > AddIns.

You also want to change the file name to something that best describes the add-in you're creating. For our example, the name will be *Bonus*.

Click the **Save** button to save the add-in.

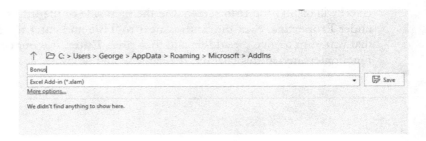

Note: Your PERSONAL.XLSB workbook remains unaffected by this save action.

10. **Next, activate your add-in in Excel Options**.

    Click **File** > **Options** > **Add-ins** to open the Add-ins pane of Excel Options.

    At the bottom of the Add-ins pane in Excel Options, ensure **Excel Add-ins** is selected in the **Manage** drop-down list box, then click the **Go** button.

    This will open the **Add-ins** dialog box.

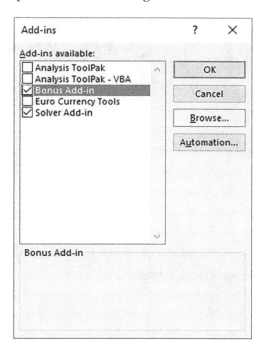

    Under **Add-ins available**, click the checkbox next to your add-in to activate it and click **OK**. This will close the Add-ins dialog box.

11. **Hide the PERSONAL.XLSB workbook again**.

    On the **View** tab, in the **Window** group, click the **Hide** command button to hide the Personal Macro Workbook again.

12. **Use your custom function in your worksheet.**

Return to the worksheet with the data you want to calculate. This should be a different workbook from the Personal Macro Workbook. You can now use your custom function by selecting the cell in which you want the result and entering its name in the formula bar.

For example:

=Bonus(B4,C4)

D4		:	×	✓	*fx*	=Bonus(B4,C4)	
◢	A		B		C	D	E
1	**Estate Agent Bonus**						
2							
3	Estate Agent		# of Rentals		Revenue	Bonus	
4	Theresa Sanchez		2		$6,176	$123.52	
5	Alice Morgan		3		$7,875	$157.50	
6	Steven Ross		4		$29,448	$588.96	
7	Craig Griffin		5		$22,178	$776.23	
8	Johnny Henderson		6		$50,882	$1,780.87	
9	Jose Baker		2		$15,920	$318.40	
10	Maria Anderson		6		$113,687	$3,979.05	
11	Henry White		7		$115,538	$4,043.83	
12	Anne Washington		1		$8,677	$130.16	
13	Wanda James		12		$228,691	$9,147.64	
14							

You user-defined function will now also appear in the Insert Function dialog box, under the User Defined category, without a prefix of the workbook name in which it was stored.

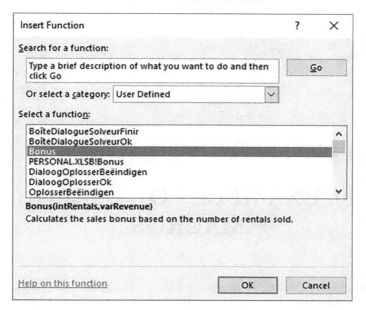

10. EXAMPLES OF USEFUL MACROS

This chapter provides a number of macro examples you can use directly in your own workbooks or seeds which you can use to build your own macros. To use the macros in this chapter in your worksheets, see the steps under the **Move Rows Up or Down** section for how to add one of these macros to an individual worksheet or your Personal Macro Workbook.

In this chapter, we will cover the following macros:
- Move rows up or down.
- Unhide all hidden rows and columns in your workbook.
- Unmerge all merged cells.
- Convert all formulas to values.
- Create banded rows in your data list.
- Convert selected cells to uppercase text.
- Highlight blank cells.
- Sort multiple columns in a data list.

Move Rows Up or Down

Let's say you have a to-do list of items in Excel, and you want to be able to move items up and down the list depending on their priority. Excel 2019, out of the box, doesn't provide a means to do this easily. You have to cut and paste a row to move it. Although this works, it can introduce errors in a larger data list because you could easily overwrite other data in the process, or even lose data.

This is where a macro that can automatically perform this function can help. For instance, the *Todo List* below is a simple list of numbered items. When you move a row up (or down) you also want the list number to change.

	A	B
1	**Todo List**	
2		
3	1	Take car to mechanic
4	2	Visit farmers market
5	3	Join local gym
6	4	DIY - fix windows
7	5	DIY - Fix computer desk
8	6	Plan family trip and get tickets
9	7	Finish course material
10	8	Call phone company
11	9	Call friend
12	10	Complete website design
13		

To achieve this aim with macros, you need two macros. One to move a row up and another to move a row down. The macro also needs to be able to change an items list number (if there is any) to match the current position of the item on the list.

RowUp

The first **If** statement in the RowUp macro checks that the active row is not the first item on the list. If it's the first row in the worksheet or the first item on a numbered list, the macro exits with a message saying the first item on the list cannot be moved up. If the active cell is not the first row or first item on the list, then the macro selects the whole row, cuts it, and inserts it one row up.

The second **If** statement checks whether the first row of the column is a numbered list. If it is, the numbers for the row that moved up and the row that moved down are swapped to reflect their new positions.

```
Sub RowUp()
    ' This procedure selects the row
    ' of the active cell and moves it up by one.

  If ActiveCell.Row <> 1 _
    And (Cells(ActiveCell.Row, 1).Value) <> 1 Then

        Selection.EntireRow.Select
        Selection.EntireRow.Cut
        Selection.Offset(-1, 0).Insert Shift:=xlDown
        Selection.Offset(-1, 0).Select

        ' Check if column one of the row
        ' contains a numbered list. If it does,
        ' then change the numbers to
        ' reflect the new positions of the rows.

        If IsNumeric(Cells(ActiveCell.Row, 1).Value) _
            And (Cells(ActiveCell.Row, 1).Value) <> "" Then

            Cells(ActiveCell.Row, 1).Value _
            = Cells(ActiveCell.Row, 1).Value - 1

            Cells(ActiveCell.Row + 1, 1).Value _
            = Cells(ActiveCell.Row + 1, 1).Value + 1
        End If
  Else
    MsgBox "Row 1 of List Cannot Be Moved Up."
  End If
End Sub
```

RowDown

The RowDown does not need to check whether the active row is the first row in the worksheet because it moved the row down. When executed, selects the row with the active cell, cuts it, and inserts it one row down.

The second part of the code checks whether the first cell of the row is a numbered list. If it is, the numbers are swapped to reflect the new row positions.

```vba
Sub RowDown()
    ' This function selects the row of the
    ' active cell and moves it down by one.

    Selection.EntireRow.Select
    Selection.EntireRow.Cut
    Selection.Offset(2, 0).Insert Shift:=xlDown
    Selection.Offset(1, 0).Select

    ' Check if column one of the row
    ' contains a numbered list. If it does,
    ' then change the numbers to
    ' reflect the new positions of the rows.

    If IsNumeric(Cells(ActiveCell.Row, 1).Value) _
        And (Cells(ActiveCell.Row, 1).Value) <> "" Then

        Cells(ActiveCell.Row, 1).Value _
        = Cells(ActiveCell.Row, 1).Value + 1

        Cells(ActiveCell.Row - 1, 1).Value _
        = Cells(ActiveCell.Row - 1, 1).Value - 1
    End If
End Sub
```

To use these macros, you can enter them in an individual worksheet, or you can enter them in the Personal Macro Workbook which will make them globally available to all worksheets on your PC.

To insert the macros in your Personal Macro Workbook, follow the steps below:

1. Open the worksheet.

2. On the **Developer** tab, in the **Code** group, click the **Visual Basic** command button to open the Visual Basic Editor.

3. In the Project Explorer window of the Visual Basic Editor, expand the tree for the Personal Address Workbook. This should be named in the format, *VBAProject(PERSONAL.XLSB)*.

4. Expand the project tree, and under the **Modules** folder, create a new module to store your macros (see the chapter on **Creating New Modules** for how to create new modules in Project Explorer).

5. Once you've created the new module, double-click on it to open its code window on the right pane and type in your code.

6. When done, click **File** > **Save** on the menu bar (or click on the **Save** button on the Visual Basic Editor toolbar).

7. On the Visual Basic Editor toolbar, click the **View Microsoft Excel** button (or press Alt+F11) to switch to Excel.

8. In Excel, create two command buttons on the Ribbon to run the RowUp and RowDown macros you've just created. The macros do not have to be local to your current Excel workbook in order for you to assign them to buttons on the Ribbon. See chapter 3 for how to assign macros to command buttons on the Ribbon.

With that, you're set. You can now click on the buttons to move items up or down your list.

To enter the code in an individual worksheet, do the following:

1. Open the worksheet.

2. On the **Developer** tab, in the **Code** group, click the **Visual Basic** command button to open the Visual Basic Editor.

3. In the Project Explorer window of the Visual Basic Editor, expand the tree for the current workbook. This should be named in the format, *VBAProject(YourWorkbookName)*.

4. Double-click on the object named ThisWorkbook to open its code window.

5. Type in your code in the code window on the right pane.

6. When done, click **File** > **Save** on the menu bar (or click on the **Save** button on the Visual Basic Editor toolbar).

7. On the Visual Basic Editor toolbar, click the **View Microsoft Excel** button (or press Alt+F11) to switch to Excel.

8. In Excel, create two command buttons on the Ribbon to run the RowUp and RowDown macros. See chapter 3 for how to assign macros to command buttons on the Ribbon.

9. Save your Excel workbook file as an Excel Macro-Enabled Workbook (.xlsm file) because it now contains macros. Note that the macros will be discarded if you save the file as a regular Excel file (.xlsx).

That's it! You can now select any cell within the list and use the command buttons to move rows up or down your list.

Unhide All Rows and Columns

This macro unhides all the hidden rows and columns. A macro like this is useful when there are several hidden rows and columns in your worksheet and you're not sure which ones are hidden. Running this macro ensures that there is no hidden data as you work on the worksheet.

```
Sub UnhideRC()
    ' Unhide all hidden rows and columns in the current
worksheet.

    Columns.EntireColumn.Hidden = False
    Rows.EntireRow.Hidden = False

End Sub
```

Unmerge All Merge Cells

If you are working in a worksheet with a lot of merge cells it can be confusing to format cells or identify what cells formulas are referencing. You can unmerge the cells manually, but it could also be very time-consuming to identify and unmerge all the merged cells in a large worksheet. A macro like this automatically identifies and unmerges all merged cells.

```
Sub UnmergeAll()
    ActiveSheet.Cells.UnMerge
End Sub
```

Convert All Formulas to Values

If you have a large data set with lots of formulas that you want to convert to ordinary values, identifying the formula cells and converting them manually can be very time-consuming. A macro like this will do it automatically for all formula cells in your worksheet. This is equivalent to copying cells with formulas and pasting them as values only.

```
Sub ConvertFormulasToValues()
'Convert all formulas in the current worksheet to values.

    With ActiveSheet.UsedRange
        .Value = .Value
    End With
End Sub
```

Create Branded Rows in Your Data List

To create banded rows in a data list or table, you highlight alternate rows in the data list. The colour separation usually makes it easier to read the data. You can use the macro below to automatically create alternate highlighting in a selected range. I've used vbCyan here, but other VBA colour constants you can use include vbBlack, vbRed, vbGreen, vbYellow, vbBlue, and vbMagenta.

```
Sub CreateBandedRows()
'Create banded rows in the selected range by highlighting
alternate rows.

    Dim objRange As Range
    Dim objRow As Range

    Set objRange = Selection
    For Each objRow In objRange.Rows
       If objRow.Row Mod 2 > 0 Then
          objRow.Interior.Color = vbCyan
       End If
    Next objRow
End Sub
```

Change Text to Uppercase

There are built-in formulas in Excel that enable you to convert strings to uppercase, lowercase, or proper case. However, you would need to insert the formula in your data, and this can be tedious if you have a lot of values to change. You can use the code below to convert values in the selected range to uppercase. The UCase function is used here, but you can also use the lowercase function LCase if you want to convert values to lowercase instead.

```vba
Sub ConvertToUpperCase()
' Convert all words in the selected range to     uppercase.

    Dim objRange As Range

    For Each objRange In Selection.Cells
        If objRange.HasFormula = False Then
            objRange.Value = UCase(objRange.Value)
        End If
    Next objRange

End Sub
```

You can use the code below to convert the selected range to Proper case (which capitalizes the first letter of each sentence).

```vba
Sub ConvertToProperCase()
'Capitalize the first letter of all words in the selected
range.

    Dim objRange As Range

    For Each objRange In Selection.Cells
        If objRange.HasFormula = False Then
            objRange.Value                              =
WorksheetFunction.Proper(objRange.Value)
        End If
    Next objRange

End Sub
```

Highlight Blank Cells

Occasionally, you may have a large worksheet with lots of data, and you want to be able to identify and mark the blank cells. This could enable you to quickly identify gaps in the data or missing values in the data set. The macro below automatically highlights all blank cells in the data list. The macro only works if there is some data present in the column, so it will not highlight cells in rows and columns with no data at all.

```
Sub HighlightBlankCells()
'Highlight all blank cells within the selected data.

    Dim objRange As Range
    Set objRange = Selection

objRange.SpecialCells(xlCellTypeBlanks).Interior.Color =
vbYellow
End Sub
```

Sort Data Using Multiple Columns

This macro will be useful to you if you often get a data list that you need to quickly sort using a number of columns. You can customize the macro for your data list. You can change which columns are used for the sort by changing the cell references in the code. In this example, A1 and B1 are used as the sort fields. You can also change the sort order by using xlDescending instead of xlAscending.

```
Sub MultiColumnSort()
' Sorts the data in cells A1:D16 in ascending order using
columns A1 and B1.

    With ActiveSheet.Sort
        .SortFields.Add              Key:=Range("A1"),
Order:=xlAscending
        .SortFields.Add              Key:=Range("B1"),
Order:=xlAscending
        .SetRange Range("A1:D10")
        .Header = xlYes
        .Apply
    End With
End Sub
```

11. GETTING MORE HELP FOR EXCEL VBA

Getting good with VBA (or any programming language for that matter) is a journey that requires time and practice. A book like this can only provide a solid platform from which you can gain that practice as you use VBA over time. The good news is that with the advent of the Internet, things have become a lot easier for programmers as we no longer need to have large volumes on our desk as reference guides for every keyword and syntax in a programming language. Now, the answer to whatever question you have is just a fingertip away using your favourite Internet search browser.

In this chapter, we will cover a couple of resources that will help you on your journey to becoming an expert VBA programmer.

Use the Macro Recorder

One of the best places to get VBA help is to use the macro recorder to record the actions you want your code to perform. When you record your actions in Excel with the macro recorder, Excel writes the underlying VBA code for you. You can then review the code to see what the recorder created and then try to customize it for your specific needs.

For example, say you want a macro that deletes multiple unwanted columns from a data list, resizes the remaining columns, and sorts the data using multiple columns. Writing this macro from scratch would be daunting if you're new to VBA. Instead, you can start the macro recorder and record yourself performing the actions. After you finish recording, you can review the code and make any necessary changes.

Use Internet Search

Back in the day, before the explosion of information on the Internet, you would need several thick and boring books by your side as reference manuals for whenever you needed help with coding a particular syntax. Now, a search engine like Google is your reference manual (after you've gone through a book like this to familiarise yourself with the basics of the language).

The reality is that there is hardly any original code anymore as pretty much every macro syntax that will ever be needed has already been written by someone somewhere and shared on the Internet. Programming has become more of deciding what you want to do and then being resourceful in finding the code syntax online that fits your particular scenario.

If you are stuck in creating a particular piece of functionality, go to your Internet search browser and type in what you are trying to do in VBA, and you will get answers. Over time, you'll become better at finding answers online for whatever you want to code in VBA.

User Forums

If you find yourself stuck, post your question to an Excel/VBA forum online to get answers more specific to your scenario.

Sharing code online actually started with online communities like user forums. User forums are online communities that focus on a particular subject of interest. You can post questions there and people who can answer it will respond. The help you get is totally free from volunteers who have a passion for the subject and wish to offer help to the community. There are many forums online dedicated to Excel and VBA.

You'll likely come across forums when you search for help on a VBA scenario you're struggling with. If you can't find an answer for your specific scenario, you can always register as a member and post your own questions.

The thing about coding is that for every challenging scenario you meet, there are usually other people online who have encountered the exact same problem and sought answers online. So, in a forum, always use the search function to check first whether your question has already been asked and answered. This can save you a lot of time. If you do post a question, be specific on what you want to do. The more specific you are, the quicker and more relevant the responses will be.

VBA Online Reference

If you are searching for something more specific, like the number and type of arguments in a particular VBA function, then you can use the VBA online help. For example, if you're looking for help with the MsgBox function, go to the language reference page (link below) and type "MsgBox" in the search bar. One of the search results will give you a detailed breakdown of all the arguments, descriptions, and examples for how to use the function.

https://docs.microsoft.com/en-us/office/vba/api/overview/language-reference

AFTERWORD

Thank you for buying and reading this book. I hope it will serve as a great Excel/VBA resource for you in the months and years to come. As mentioned in the introduction, this is an introductory Excel programming book, hence, the topics have been kept at a level to ensure someone who has not even written a line of code before can find it useful. If you have any comments or suggestions for how this book can be improved even further, please feel free to contact me at **info@excelbytes.com**.

INDEX

ABOUT THE AUTHOR

Nathan George is a computer science graduate with several years' experience in the IT services industry in different roles, including Excel programming and providing end-user support to Excel power users. One of his main interests is using computers to automate tasks and increase productivity. As an author, he has written several technical and non-technical books.

OTHER BOOKS BY AUTHOR

Excel 2019 Basics

A Quick and Easy Guide to Boosting Your Productivity with Excel

Excel 2019 Basics covers all the essentials you need to quickly get up to speed in creating spreadsheets solutions for your data.

If you are new to Excel and the thought of spreadsheets makes your head spin, then this is the right book for you. This book will hold your hand through a step-by-step process in becoming skilled with Excel.

If you already have some Excel skills and you want to skill-up on more advanced topics like functions, Excel tables, charts, and pivot tables then this book is also for you. *Excel 2019 Basics* goes beyond introductory topics and covers topics like functions, Excel tables, and analysing your data with charts.

The aim of this book is to guide you from beginner to being skilled with Excel within a few short hours.

For more information, please visit:

https://www.excelbytes.com/excel-books/

Excel 2019 Advanced Topics

Leverage More Powerful Tools to Enhance Your Productivity

Whether you have basic Excel skills or you're a power user, *Excel 2019 Advanced Topics* is full of methods and tips that will enable you to take advantage of more powerful tools in Excel to boost your productivity.

Excel 2019 Advanced Topics covers a selection of advanced topics relevant to productivity tasks you're more likely to perform at home or at work. This book does not only show you how to use specific features but also in what context those features need to be used.

Excel 2019 Advanced Topics explains how to automate Excel with macros, use What-If Analysis tools to create alternate data scenarios and projections, analyze data with pivot tables and pivot charts, debug formulas, solve complex data scenarios with advanced functions, use data tools to consolidate data, remove duplicate values from lists, create financial formulas to carry out financial calculations, and much more.

For more information, please visit:

https://www.excelbytes.com/excel-books/

Excel 2019 Functions

70 Top Excel Functions Made Easy

Do you want to delve more into Excel functions and leverage their full power in your formulas?

Excel functions are predefined formulas that make it easier and faster to create solutions for your data.

Excel 2019 Functions provides a detailed coverage of 70 of the most useful and relevant Excel functions in various categories including logical, reference, statistical, financial, math, and text functions.

Learn how to use many advanced functions introduced in Excel 2016/2019 like the IFS function which can replace convoluted nested IF functions. This book also comes with lots of Excel examples which you can download as Excel files, so you can copy and use the formulas in your own worksheets. *Excel 2019 Functions* will be a great resource for you whether you're a beginner or experienced with Excel.

For more information, please visit:

https://www.excelbytes.com/excel-books/

CPSIA information can be obtained
at www.ICGtesting.com
Printed in the USA
FSHW020753090820
72814FS

9 781916 211346